Dedication

FOR THOSE WHO MUST SAIL

Text © 2016 by Roger Vaughan

Project directors: Gary Jobson, Malcolm Page
Art Direction: Roger Vaughan
Design: Fiona Edwards

Published in 2016 by
World Sailing
Ariadne House, Town Quay
Southampton SO14 2AQ
United Kingdom

Library of Congress Cataloging-in-Publication Data

Vaughan, Roger
Emerging Nations Program / Roger Vaughan
Foreword by Robert Scheidt

ISBN 978-0-9568091-2-4
1. Youth Sailing – UK

The text of this book was composed in Bodoni MT Regular
Captions were composed in Futura Standard

Printed and bound in Italy by Papergraf

10 9 8 7 6 5 4 3 2 1

First Printing
2016

CLOSING THE   GAP

World Sailing's
Emerging Nations Program

By ROGER VAUGHAN

Introduction by
GARY JOBSON

Foreword by
ROBERT SCHEIDT

Photographs by

Chris Cameron   Daniel Forster   Trevor Wilkins
Carlo Borlenghi   Christophe Launay

CONTENTS

Because We Must

By Gary Jobson

A compelling element of any sporting competition captured on film is the ability to see the emotions expressed on the athletes faces. Photographs of the young sailors in CLOSING THE GAP, World Sailing's Emerging Nations Program, tell an engaging story about the rigors of our sport. Determination, frustration, sweat, exuberance, satisfaction, and joy are all on display.

Those of us who sail do so because we must. It is our compulsion, and it lasts a lifetime. That's why friendships formed among sailors endure. For many young people, being in control of a sailboat is their initial brush with leadership and teamwork. Sailing offers freedom, teaches respect for the environment. Competition accelerates the learning process. With the counsel of skilled coaches and the support of dedicated mentors, sailors will improve their sailing skills and look forward to spending many enjoyable years on the water. Many will aspire to compete in the Olympic Games. Some will attain that goal.

The common denominator for this inspiring narrative is water. Boats and water are the elements that transcend language, political, and cultural barriers, and bring sailors together from around the world. As you read author Roger Vaughan's words, and appreciate the moments captured by our cadre of superb photographers, put yourself in the boats with these young sailors. Our tapestry of reportage is woven of mistakes and disappointments as well as triumphs. Think back to your own early days on the water and recall how every hour offered tests that built your confidence, how your appreciation for the water grew.

As someone who has sailed for 60 years, I never race without learning something. Refining one's skills never ends in this life sport. After one of these ENP clinics, young sailors will begin to grasp this marvelous truth.

World Sailing President Carlo Croce and his seven vice presidents have all had vital roles in this project. Nazli Imre from Turkey has spent eight years overseeing the Youth World Championship. Greece's George Andreadis has long been a champion of building sailing in remote regions of the world. W. Scott Perry, of Uruguay, has been at the forefront of nurturing sailing in South America. Adrienne Greenwood, from New Zealand, helped bring the 2016

Youth World Championships to her country. Walking through the boat park in Qingdao with Quanhai Li, I was impressed that he knew the names of every competitor we visited at the Sailing World Cup in China. Chris Atkins has worked diligently to improve the overall quality of racing and race management around the world. My contribution was to produce this book and the accompanying documentary. President Croce is a two-time Olympian who has experienced every level of sailing. All of us are beneficiaries of his leadership.

In the coming years you will likely hear about many of the young sailors mentioned in this book: sailing in the Olympics, competing in 'round-the-world races, or winning major championships. Their responsibility will be to pass their knowledge and enthusiasm on to the next generation. That should come naturally.

Twice College Sailor of the Year and America's Cup winning tactician, Gary Jobson is a World Sailing Vice President, television commentator, and author.

Gary Jobson sailing a Laser (1972).

Robert Scheidt and his sister play in his Laser, age 13 (1980).

Foreword

by Robert Scheidt

I started sailing because of my father. When I was five, I was crewing for him on Lake Guarapiranga near Sao Paulo, Brazil, in a family boat. When I was nine, I took an Opti course at the local yacht club. I was lucky because the club had a strong sailing history. We had several Olympic champions in the 1960s, 1970s, and 1980s, sailors who were mentors for us younger, aspiring sailors.

In emerging nations, there is not such a strong background of sailing. This is true even in northern Brazil. It is warm there year round, and the sailing conditions are exceptional, but they don't have the necessary people and programs. It is important to bring experienced people into these places to give young sailors an opportunity to shorten the learning curve by many years.

Sailing is a great sport because boats can accommodate people of both sexes, and of all ages, sizes, levels of fitness and endurance, and technical know-how.
Sailing is also a complex sport because you have to deal with so many variables. You might start in a singlehanded boat, then go into a doublehanded boat where you have to learn to communicate with a fellow crewman. And you have to constantly adapt to different conditions, especially as you travel to regattas. If you don't have access to the sport's state-of-the-art resources, from boats and equipment to rigging and sailing technique, you will never acquire the flexibility you need to constantly improve.

And now there is professionalism. In my first Olympic campaign in 1996, there were many people who were studying and also sailing, or working and also sailing. I graduated university just two months before I went to the Games. Now, in the bigger countries like France, Great Britain, Australia, New Zealand, and the United States, sailing for Olympic hopefuls has become a full-time job. If we don't help countries who do not have the resources to support their sailors full-time, the performance divide between the bigger and smaller countries will become ever larger. That goes against the objective of the International Olympic Committee, which is to have sports in the Games played by as many countries as possible.

I fully support World Sailing's Emerging Nation's Program. It's a great initiative that should be sustained. Expertise in this complex sport must be shared to encourage the development of champions from a wide variety of countries.

Robert Scheidt, has won five Olympic medals (silver and bronze in the Star; two gold and a silver in the Laser) and nine Laser World Championships. At age 43, he represented Brazil in the Laser Class in the 2016 Olympics

SAILING

is almost as old as life on Earth.

Early man's observation of a leaf sliding across a puddle of water must have been intriguing. Or perhaps he caught sight of a stonefly (*Plecoptera*), above, skimming across the water while holding its wings up as sails to increase speed. Historians tell us that sailing's origins may date as far back as the 5th or 6th millennium BC in Mesopotamia, but the stonefly was tacking downwind long before that.

Man walked before he sailed, but that's the only form of transportation that preceded sailing. The wheel didn't come along until ca.3500 BC. Quite a few years before that (60,000 BC, some say), the Polynesians had discovered and colonized thousands of Pacific islands in their sailing canoes and outriggers. Sailing unlocked the gates of the world, providing a vehicle for man's inborn, insatiable curiosity about what was across the river, or beyond the horizon. Sailing took fishermen to more productive waters, and ferried travelers to otherwise inaccessible destinations. It wasn't long before competition entered the picture, competition to bring a catch of fish to a small village, for instance. We all know that two sailboats within sight of one another is the definition of a race. One must assume that definition was born the very first time it happened. It was inevitable that sailing would eventually become a sport.

The basic tactics of competitive sailing were invented and refined in naval combat, beginning with the Egyptians. From the outset, speed was a critical element of victory at sea, as it was for success in trade. The need for maneuverability quickly followed. It was just a matter of time before men of means were challenging one another to duels under sail, with substantial wagers riding on the outcome. Several yacht clubs in the United States were founded in the 1840s, including the New York Yacht Club in 1844, with a condition for membership being ownership of a large yacht. Russia's Imperial Yacht Club, whose members were drawn exclusively from the aristocracy, dates to 1846. The first America's Cup race took place in 1851. The St. Petersburg River Yacht Club in Russia was founded in 1860. The club excluded anyone who had ever worked for wages.

By 1888, sailing tactics were firmly established in the lexicon. The Encyclopedic Dictionary, published that year, defined taking the wind out of someone's sails as depriving them of their means of progress, "as by one vessel sailing between the wind and another vessel."

When a sport is born, standardized rules of play must follow. Probably no sport relies tactically on the rules as much as sailing. Unlike other games played on well-defined, hard surfaces with object balls or discs, goals, and a set number of players often wearing numbered uniforms,

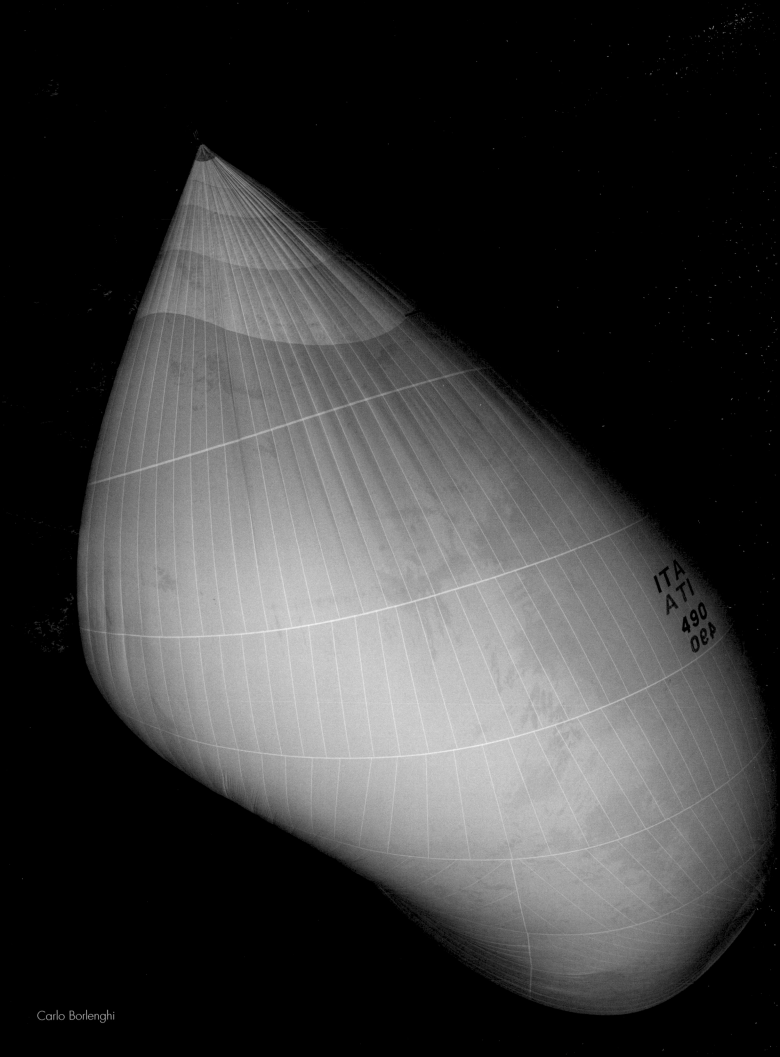

Carlo Borlenghi

"I have never met a dumb sailor"

sailors compete on a vast, unstable medium (water) with a second unstable medium (wind) providing their power. As a result, sailors are at the whim of Mother Nature, and she abides by her own complicated rules. From that fact alone, perhaps one can begin to comprehend the diversified knowledge, the depth of understanding, the fitness, and the adventuresome spirit that competitive sailing requires. A sailor must begin with a basic comprehension of both aero- and fluid dynamics that explain why sailboats work. Next, sailors board a vessel of choice and manipulate scores of lines that shape mast and sails for optimum speed given ever-changing conditions ranging from gear-breaking gales to flat calms. They do it in temperatures ranging from sweltering to freezing, usually while working on a tilt and being jolted by random bumps. Meanwhile, in the cockpit, the skipper's job is to steer the fastest course possible while his tactician plans strategic moves and communicates with the crew. As a former top sailing administrator once said, "Sailors may do dumb things, but I have never met a dumb sailor."

The initial rules for sailboats were written in the interest of avoiding collision, basically copying the rules for motorways. Since sailboats cannot make progress pointing directly into the wind, boats underway must always be on one "tack" or the other – port (wind on the left side, sails on the right), or starboard (wind on the right side, sails on the left) – with starboard tack always having the right of way.

That's where the simplicity of the rules ends, because obstructions and the traffic of other boats seeking advantage by "playing" the rules to gain right-of-way positions enter the picture. Situations often arise in fleet racing that can require trained legal minds and judges to resolve. And since boats tend to be different from one another, except in one-design fleets, there are also rules for design, construction, and the complexity of handicapping – a puzzle combining higher mathematics and actual and predicted performance that is yet to be satisfactorily solved after more than 100 years.

Finally, because sailors tend to be an innovative lot, from designers to on-the-water tacticians, and because technology regularly advances the strength-to-weight ratio of materials used in construction of hulls, masts, lines, sails, and gear, the rules have to constantly be re-written to keep up with new loopholes (progress!) that are discovered. In 1945, the rules of sailing were set down in a stapled pamphlet of 14 pages. In 2015, the Racing Rules of Sailing is a 180-page, ring-bound book.

Before 1870, early yacht clubs wrote their own rules, which made racing against other clubs an uncertain undertaking. Committees were formed, measurement standards were hotly debated, but little progress was made until 1907, when the International Yacht Racing Union (IYRU) was formed and adopted the first Racing Rules of Sailing that was being used by the Yacht Racing Association of Great Britain. In 1929, the North American Yacht Racing Union (NAYRU) and the IYRU got together and ensured

Daniel Forster

that the rules they both lived by were virtually identical. Harold Vanderbilt led a group that began writing the "Vanderbilt Rules" in 1930, But it wasn't until 1960 that a totally universal code of racing rules was globally implemented.

In 1996, IYRU became the International Sailing Federation (ISAF). At the end of 2015, ISAF became World Sailing, a name that better describes its global oversight of the sport of sailing. Consisting of 139 member nations, World Sailing promotes sailing as a sport; trains and certifies judges, umpires, and administrators; represents sailors in all matters concerning the sport; sanctions all major regattas including the Olympics, Paralympics, and the America's Cup; and develops the sport around the world. In his 2016 re-election manifesto, President Carlo Croce added this to World Sailing's goals: become a world leader in ocean sustainability.

It was the development part of World Sailing's franchise that took a step forward in 2015 with the activation of the Emerging Nations Program (ENP), an effort aimed at narrowing the performance gap between elite sailing nations like Australia, France, New Zealand, the United Kingdom, and the United States, and emerging sailing nations like Antigua, Fiji, and Malaysia. That gap is substantial. In the last 20 years, all sports at the Olympic and professional levels have made huge advances in performance, thanks to constant refinements in equipment, fitness, nutrition, and coaching techniques that place more emphasis on psychology. Sailing is no exception. Victor Kovalenko, head and 470 coach of the Australian Olympic sailing team, a man who has steered teams to more Olympic medals than any coach in history, has said the way top teams are sailing today makes the standard of ten, even five years ago seem like the dark ages. But keeping up with developments that lead to top performance takes international participation (travel), excellent coaching, a good organization or system, and funding. The equipment and logistics required for sailing are a bit more challenging than dealing with a ball and a pair of sneakers.

ISAF created the position of Training

Development Manager in 2009. Dan Jaspers, a sailor, certified dinghy coach, and secondary-school teacher (outdoor education and art), was hired to fill the job described as working to increase participation in sailing around the globe. In the course of six years Jaspers traveled to more than 50 countries, taking stock of sailing talent, availability of boats and gear, facilities, coach development programs, and scholarships, and making connections and friends. He developed a color code for categorizing countries. Red was for the haves, the elite nations. Orange indicated countries whose sailors occasionally made it to international events. Green indicated totally emerging programs.

More than a ball and a pair of sneakers

"Sailing was going on," says Jaspers, who left ISAF in 2015, "but in the emerging nations there were no training programs, no nationally structured programs, no momentum, no follow-up; just a few independently wealthy families supporting their kids. Or a country would invest heavily in one talented athlete with no sustained strategy in mind.

"I wanted to track sailors," Jaspers says. "Why do they drop out? Because there is no pathway, no guidance, no financial help. If we have to start with different people every year, if the ones we have invested in don't come back, it doesn't work. If the sailor is keen, if you are coaching him well, he or she should stay in the sport. We don't call these people athletes. An athlete is a full-time professional sports person. These sailors aren't paid, they are not training full-time. We mustn't force them into a category they aren't ready for."

Just a year after Dan Jaspers joined ISAF, Antonio González de la Madrid joined the organization as Competition Manager, in charge of Team and Match Racing as well as the annual Youth World Championships. The two men ended up sharing a flat, and talking at length about their roles in ISAF and how they could collaborate. "Both of us," González de la Madrid says, "wanted to increase participation and legacy. It wasn't just

18

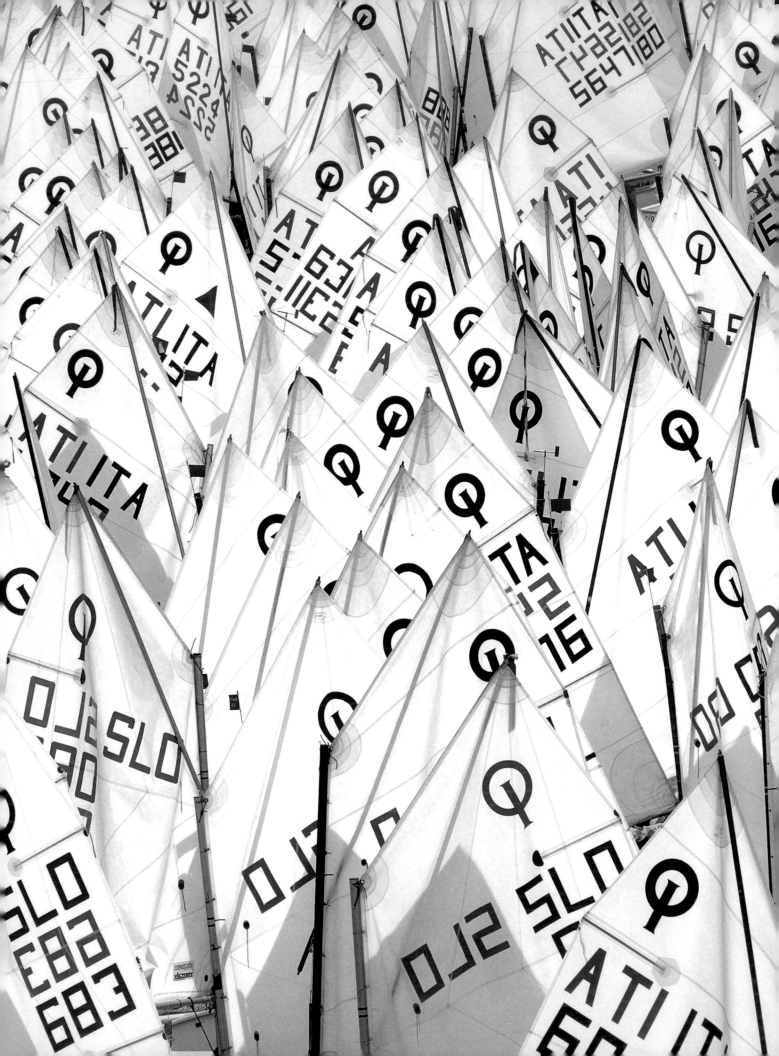

getting sailors to the Youth Worlds, it was keeping them interested and competing beyond that."

Based on what he'd learned, Jaspers' emphasis became two-fold. One was to encourage grassroots, entry-level sailing. "In some countries that would be performance-based," he says, "competition and racing. Or it could be school children coming into the sport for the first time." The second was not only to infuse emerging nations with expertise delivered in regional clinics, but also to provide organized pathways sailors could choose to follow to international and (ultimately) Olympic competition.

The collaboration between Jaspers and González de la Madrid resulted in the first Emerging Nations Program being connected to the 2011 ISAF Sailing World Championships in Perth, Australia. "It was so successful," González de la Madrid says, "we repeated it in Santander, Spain, the next year. Now it is part of the requirement for hosting the Worlds. It's always been funded by the organizers and ISAF. The idea is simple: run clinics in different parts of the world, grant scholarships to sailors identified by their countries, and finish the program with a clinic for them at the host venue the year of the championship."

True, the idea was simple, and proved effective. The question was how to run a similar program in association with the Youth Worlds. ISAF had something called the Athletes Participation Program (APP) in place that helped a few sailors get to the Youth Worlds by funding part of their travel expenses and entry fees. But APP was woefully underfunded given the demands on it.

A Youth Worlds Emerging Nations Program finally materialized in late 2014 when Gazprom, the leading Russian energy conglomerate, came forward with a sizable donation to World Sailing. "Gazprom wanted to get involved with youth," World Sailing president Carlo Croce says. "Many of their executives are keen sailors with big yachts, and they remember how they got started."

Encourage grass-roots entry-level sailing

Carlo Borlenghi

The ENP for youth had been so pre-organized, so primed, that full activation happened within months. Locations for the week-long clinics had been selected based on their organizer's ability to provide a sufficient number of boats, a reasonable sailing facility, nearby accommodations, proximity to an international airport, and the ability to deliver the program at an affordable cost. The five venues selected would engage a total of 68 countries. Fiji was host for the South Pacific region. Hungary hosted the Western Asian and Eastern European countries. Mozambique, in the southern sub-Saharan region, was the center for African sailors. Antigua represented the Caribbean and Americas regions from North and South America. Malaysia, home of the 2015 Youth World Championships, hosted the Eastern Asian clinic. In each venue, sailors and coaches gathered from as many as 20 countries. World Sailing covered 50% of everyone's plane fare up to a maximum of $600 USD. Lodging, food, and the chartering of boats were also underwritten by World Sailing. Two "nominated experts" (sailing coaches/teachers) were dispatched by World Sailing to organize and run each event. Scholarships were in place that would help send the most accomplished sailors, selected by their various

countries, to the Youth Worlds. Some of the world's most respected photographers and videographers were also contracted by World Sailing to record all five events, and to make this book and a film possible. Typically, the week-long programs consisted of daily classroom sessions alternating with on-the-water drills that stressed specific aspects of racing. A regatta was held the final two days. Dan Jaspers attended the first ENP clinic in Fiji. After six long years, he says it was difficult to believe it was actually happening. "But we had the sailors there, and the boats, and the coaches, and our experts, and after a couple days it was rolling and for me that was the reality. The energy around all the venues has been so amazing that it will be daunting to replicate it. But we have funding in place for five years, and I can only see it flourishing if we get extra support from other sponsors who identify putting money into a youth program as almost a social responsibility. We need to add equipment grants to some nations because their boats and gear are so tired the sailors can't tune them properly to maximize performance on the water. I can see a lot of scope for the growth of the Emerging Nations Program."

Carlo Borlenghi

FIJI

Fiji

Including Cook Islands, Guam, Papua New Guinea, Samoa, and Vanuatu

Photographs by Trevor Wilkins

The six countries that participated in the Emerging Nations Program in May 2015, held in Suva, Fiji, are located within Melanesia, Micronesia, or Polynesia. But all of them are part of Oceania, more than 10,000 islands scattered in the Central and South Pacific, population sixteen million if you don't count Australia and New Zealand. Oceania is one of the places on Earth where civilization took root, where exploration and colonization went on tens of thousands of years ago, under sail. Today, thanks mainly to the remoteness of the six Oceania nations listed above, and (consequently) the lack of competitive boats, gear, and coaches, the young sailors who live there are considered to be "emerging" when it comes to the sophistication required for racing boats at an international level.

Fiji and its environs definitely qualify as "paradise" when that elusive fantasy is discussed. Their waters are blue, clear, unspoiled. Their coral-sand beaches are stunning. Temperatures are in the 80s year-round. Their skies are the bluest, their clouds the whitest and fluffiest. The rain can be hard but it never lasts long, and there is always plenty of wind. But, as it should be, getting to Paradise is a journey, and distance costs time and money. Just the brief flight from Suva (Fiji's capital) to Savusavu on the island of Vanua Levu 100 miles to the northeast, for example, costs around $300 USD. Flying from Suva to Sydney, Australia, takes five hours and costs around $1000 round trip. Los Angeles to Suva is a 5,500-mile trip. London to Suva is twice that distance and more than three times the price. Oceania is a very big place.

Remoteness breeds brotherhood. "In the Pacific culture," Shane Brodie says, "everyone gets on. We're all good friends. I have a friend in Tahiti I only see every two or three years, and we are very close." Brodie, who ran the Emerging Nations Program in Suva, is head of the Fiji Yachting Association. He moved to the island in 1979 when his father started a construction company there. Brodie now runs the company when he isn't racing his Hobie 18.

Brodie says meeting World Sailing's ENP requirements was a struggle. "The only time a Pacific Island country has the money to buy boats is when it hosts the Pacific Games," Brodie says, "which are every four years, like the Olympics. The equipment is always funded by the host country. Fiji hosted in 2003, so our boats are 12 years old, and no one has had the money to maintain them. We were supposed to have 20 boats on the water. We got 12 Laser Radial hulls together, then imported parts from the US and the UK to get those boats up and running. Fortunately, several local companies came in as sponsors."

Accommodations weren't as difficult. Families are strong in Fiji. One woman, a sailor from Savusavu who now lives in Suva, invited all 18 kids to stay at her house. They brought sleeping bags and happily spread them on the floor. That attitude was one of the things that impressed Tim Cross, the Nominated Expert from World Sailing who ran the event. "No one on those islands takes anything for granted," Cross said. "Everything is appreciated. We're used to having a launching trolley for every boat. They're not. Launching just takes more time and they all help each other, working as a team lifting boats.

I Insisted they have Wi-Fi

"The clinic was hampered a little by not having a boat for every sailor," Cross said. "When we got to the regatta on the final two days, we had to sail a round robin in flights of six boats. As a result, we had half the kids as spectators cheering for those racing. That wasn't the primary vision of the outcome desired for the clinic, but it was a great thing, unique.

"The harmony among kids was greater in Fiji than any other venue, and it was strong at all of them. They'd arrive in the morning and come in to the classroom sessions with arms linked, shoving each other good-naturedly, completely cross-nationality. The clinic did so much beyond improving their sailing."

One thing that helped was the presence of Wi-Fi at the sailing center, which was just a five-minute ride from where the sailors stayed. "I insisted there be Wi-Fi," Shane Brodie says. "The kids were non-stop on social media, hashtagging everything. There were 500 more hits a day than normal."

Sailing, among the general population in Oceania, is more old tradition than current pastime. There's little sailing going on at the grassroots level. Lack of access to boats and gear is, in fact, the major problem. Perhaps led and inspired by individuals among them with an affinity for the water, today's young sailors experiment and learn from one another. "They just don't have any experts around," says Yves Simard, the videographer for the Fiji event. "They are on a journey to rediscover their roots, tapping into their own culture. They told me their grandfathers used to sail, and now they are getting into it because competitive sailing is fun. They said it was difficult to encourage their

Sailors at play. One has to remember these aspiring world and Olympic champions are still kids, ages thirteen to eighteen.

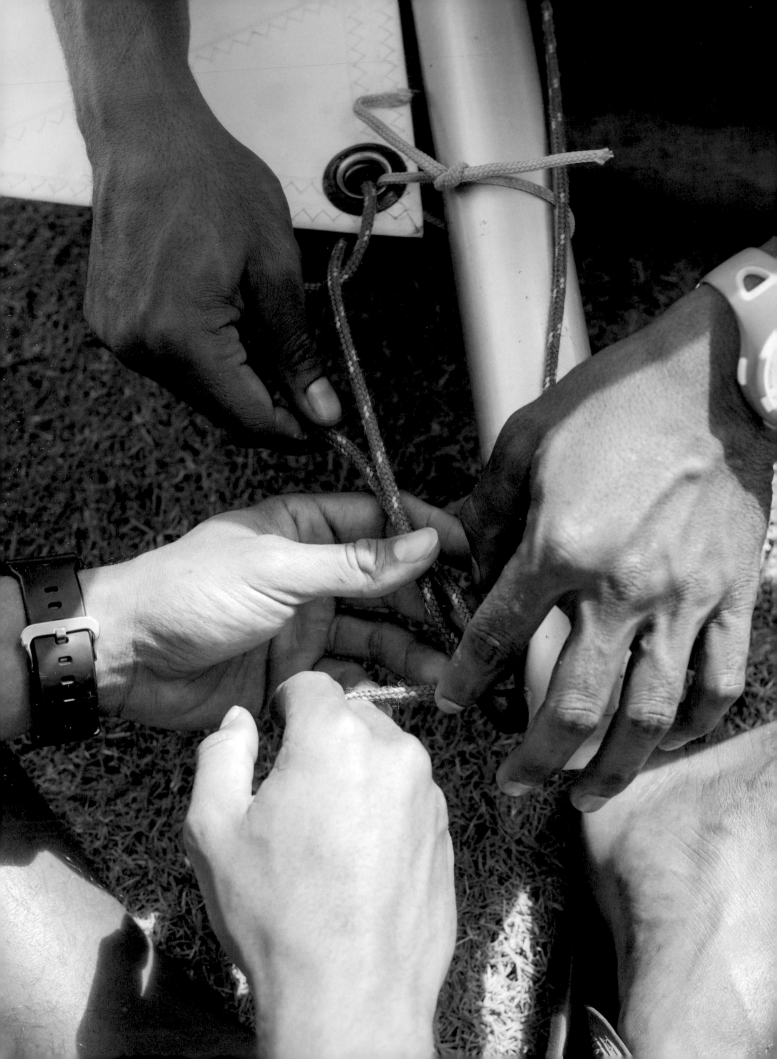

friends to join them. But with this program, here they were having a concentrated week with top-end people. They were kids in a candy store. Without this program, progress would be stagnant."

Cross said the days were long. An hour-long debriefing followed the afternoon sailing program, and by the time the boats were put away and the kids were gone Cross found himself leaving the sailing venue as late as 7:30 pm. He says he didn't get to see much of paradise. Although, one morning a fellow named John Philp, vice president of the Fiji Surfing Association, got Cross up at the crack of dawn and took him to a break outside the main harbor. They watched the sun rise and caught a few waves before the classroom session began.

She started with nothing but a dream

One morning the classroom was treated to a visit by three-time sailboard Olympic medalist Barbara Kendall, from New Zealand. Kendall was in town for a meeting of the Oceania National Olympic Committee. "She was awesome," Yves Simard says. "She told the kids she started out with no money, nothing except a dream, and she became a gold-medal board sailor. She really got them excited. She told them they had better support and training here than she'd ever had. She put a spark in them. When she got through, those kids were thinking they could go to the Olympics."

Tim Cross and his fellow Nominated Expert, Andrew Clouston from New Zealand, were surprised by the quality and intensity of the young sailors they worked with. Yves Simard says as a group the kids were confident, way past basic-level sailing and into the dynamics of racing. And they took the week

The clinic began with basics. Even rigging the boat involved some new tricks and improvements to be learned by the local sailors

of training seriously, eager to soak up better and more successful ways of handling the boats and trimming, and applying strategy and tactics. The coaches who accompanied the sailors from each country also worked hard, and departed with a useful tool: a standardized plan certified by World Sailing for how to advance themselves as coaches, and grow their sport back home.

"One minute you're giving feedback to some sailors," Tim Cross says. "The next minute you're looking at their coaches and the styles and skills they have, helping them reflect upon how they might develop those skills, and then you're working with coach and sailor together to make sure they are developing a good relationship. Training coaches is important. You can train one sailor to sail, but if you train a coach you've trained a whole bunch of sailors. The big goal," Cross says, "is for emerging nations to establish their own sustainable programs. That way, sailing will find a footing and start to reestablish itself."

"The kids were great," Shane Brodie says, "and what they got out of the ENP event was very valuable. I saw a big difference in the sailors between when they were here and I saw them again three months later at the Pacific Games. Both their boat handling and confidence were much improved. Just one week working with experts brought about really big changes."

"The sailors in Fiji took nothing for granted, including boat trolleys" Tim Cross observed "They were used to helping each other. I loved that attitude."

"People can take what they learn here home and develop it and then we can get bigger fleets, get more coaches involved, and hold more regattas."

Sydney Pettitt (VAN), Sailor

> **Knowing this is the first Emerging Nations Program and there's going to be one in the Caribbean and one in Malaysia and it's all over the world it's like, wow! I'm a part of this.**
>
> Vanic Teina (COK) Sailor

"One of the things I've taken away from this week is the bond the young sailors have developed between themselves.

What's going to bring young people into sailing and make them stay in the sport is the realization that it's a very sociable sport that brings people together.

I can see over a period of time that in perhaps 4-5 years, maybe 10 years' time there may well be sailors from these clinics we'll be observing at the front of their Olympic classes.

If there was one thing I could have all these sailors walk away from these clinics with it would be, sailing is fun."

Tim Cross, Nominated Expert

Every day of every clinic begins with stretching and fitness exercises. In Fiji, it was also old home week (left) for the kids bonded by Oceania. Nominated Expert Tim Cross (right) always had time to answer a sailor's questions.

" At first I was scared because I thought some people were better than me, but in the end I was better. I was scared of doing the races because there were kids catching up, but I was having better speed as well.

This is my first competition in the Laser Radials. I'm really new to this. I'm proud of myself for sticking with it. "

Helene Johnson Cook Islands

 Many of the young sailors have already achieved beyond their expectations. Some are capible of going a lot further, and they had no idea they could do that "

John Tierney, Secretary General Oceania Sailing Federation

47

Tim Cross announces the day's schedule that begins with classroom sessions (page opposite). A surprise appearance by New Zealand's three-time Olympic medalist Barbara Kendall (above), inspired the sailors.

The Laser learning curve includes capsizing. It takes patience, strength and technique to get the darn thing upright and keep it that way. Capsize drill is part of every ENP clinic.

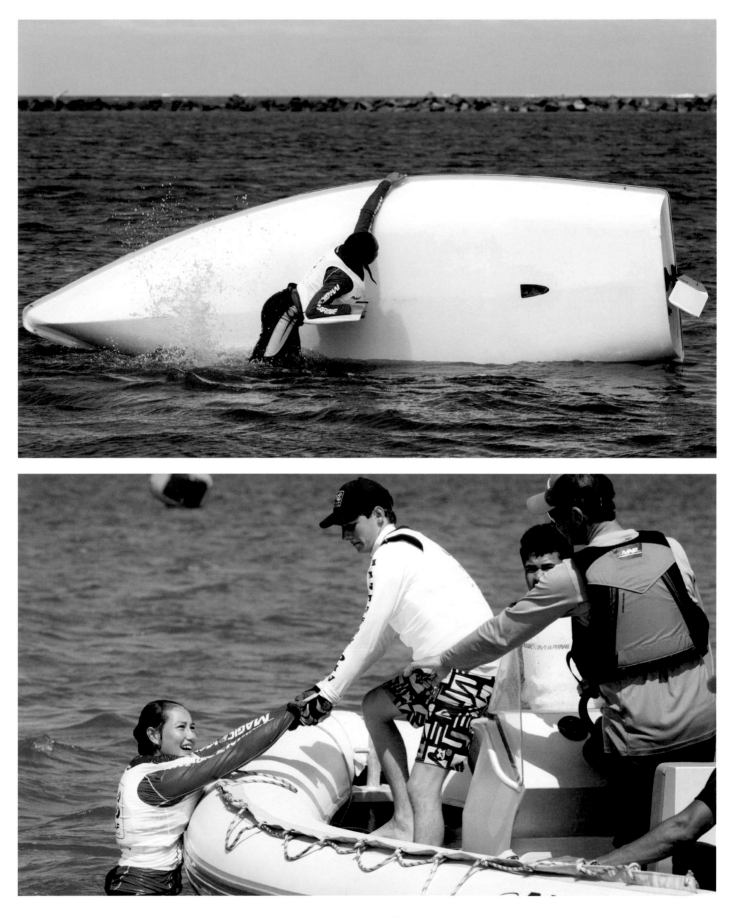

Kava root (above, and bottom page opposite) or *Piper Methysticum,* is painstakingly ground with water into Fiji's national drink. Kava is an essential of Fijian hospitality, an expected gift for all ocassions. The fertile islands also produce a variety of delicious fruits and root vegetables.

Viliame Ratulu
A Day in the Life

Geoff Taylor, who runs the Copra Shed Marina at Savusavu on the island of Vanua Levu, 100 miles northeast of Suva, has coached young sailors for 25 years. In that time, Taylor says he has seen three sailors with pure, raw talent. Vili is the latest one.

Talent just remains dormant if it isn't discovered and nourished. It requires opportunity, with environment often being a critical factor. The fact that Vanua Levu is surrounded by water is lucky for Vili. But the extreme, mid-Pacific remoteness of the little island is not a help. Neither is the fact that sailing as sport has only been available there for the last 20 years. Unlike other Fijian islands (the Lau group, 200 miles east of Suva), Vanua Levu does not have a rich sailing heritage from the period of exploration. As Vili points out, no one in his family has sailed, besides him, and that happened by accident. An athletic boy born and raised on Vanua Levu, Vili was enjoying the sea, diving and swimming, and also the land, playing Rugby Sevens, a sport at which Fijians excel. A couple of his friends were sailing, and a few Optis were both available, and free, so he tried it and discovered that not only was it great fun, but he was good at it.

"He showed exceptional talent from the outset," says Geoff Taylor, who likes Vili's strong will to win, and his intensity. "Prior to the starting sequence, it's all fun for these sailors," Taylor says. "Once the gun goes, it's all business. After the finish, it's back to the easy island way. But Vili has to stick with it. Practicing every day doesn't come easy."

Practicing every day isn't even a possibility for Vili, who like all Savusavu kids his age (16) is busy taking out the trash, washing his clothes, cleaning the house, feeding the pigs, and going to school. He gets to sail Saturday afternoons, weather permitting. In the Pacific, occasional cyclones disrupt the most committed schedule. Winston, the strongest cyclone ever to hit Fiji, did so on February 20, 2016. The harbor at Savusavu recorded winds of 145 mph. Many houses were flattened by waves driven by the storm surge.

Strong and varied competition, the essential ingredients of improvement, are also lacking in Fiji. In 2010, after three years in Optis, Vili won the national championship, the moment, he says, "when sailing became my favorite sport." But he needs more exposure to good sailors and advanced techniques, as he learned during the ENP clinic. Helene Johnson, from the Cook Islands, won every race. Vili finished second in the regatta. "She is really good," Vili says, shaking his head.

"Helene lives and trains in Australia," Geoff Taylor says. "She's very skilled, and that's the point. Vili needs to race and train in overseas fleets. Getting kids to various places is tough

because of the travel cost. But we work at it because we know that getting them to the next level requires exposure overseas."

Taylor says the ENP clinic was a huge step in that direction. "Bringing sailors, coaches, and experts to us is more efficient," Taylor says. "Vili met a lot of other kids and learned a ton from everyone. He's still texting with them, and has new friends on the internet to compare notes with. That's the sort of thing we need."

Vili's readiness to share strategic ideas (page opposite), and have a good laugh (above) makes him a popular boy.

Hungary

Including Ukraine, Czech Republic, Latvia, Slovakia, Bulgaria, Romania, Cypress, and Portugal

Photographs by Carlo Borlenghi

On May 9, 2015, 29 sailors and 11 coaches from the nine countries listed above descended on the town of Balatonfüred, Hungary, for a strenuous, one-week racing clinic sponsored by World Sailing's Emerging Nations Program. Of the five ENP events, this one at Balatonfüred was by far the most upscale. Photographer Carlo Borlinghi, who traveled to the event from Milan, was surprised by what greeted him. "I came here 15 years ago to cover an ice boating event," Borlinghi says, "and there was nothing here. Nothing."

Located on 50-mile-long Lake Balaton, a 90-minute drive from Budapest, Balatonfüred has long been a tourist attraction known for its gentle, Mediterranean climate. Several impressive mansions remain from the early days when the nobility came to take the area's healing waters. In the 18th century, during the Reform Era, it was favored by artists and progressive politicians whose presence spurred development. There was a long period of Balatonfüred being its quiet, unassuming self, but in the last dozen or so years, Balatonfüred has "exploded," according to András Holczhauser, General Secretary of the Hungarian Yachting Association, who organized the ENP clinic. There are now 80 yacht clubs on the lake, upon which power boats are prohibited save for those of coaches and police. Luxury

hotels, lounges, and restaurants have sprung up in great numbers. Population soars from 13,500 in winter to near 60,000 in season.

The ENP clinic was held at the recently completed Balatonfüred Yacht Club. Sailors were housed at a hotel within walking distance. This was also the largest clinic of the five sponsored by World Sailing because of several young local sailors who asked to be included. "That was fine with us," said nominated expert Pedro Rodrigues, from Portugal, who ran the clinic with Tim Cross. "The more boats, the better for practicing fleet management, especially starts. But of course our focus on individual progress was on the sailors who were in the clinic." There were also a couple additional "coach-experts" on hand because of having 29er (3 boats) and 420 (10 boats) fleets in addition to Laser Radials.

There was a lot to get done in seven days, so Cross and Rodrigues ran a tight program. "Watching them was impressive," event videographer George Johns said. "They didn't cut corners. If it were gray and rainy, so what, they made the most of every minute of every day. They taught kids how to communicate among themselves. Watching them I saw the difference between coaching and teaching. Coaches can be on the secretive side. Teachers share everything they know."

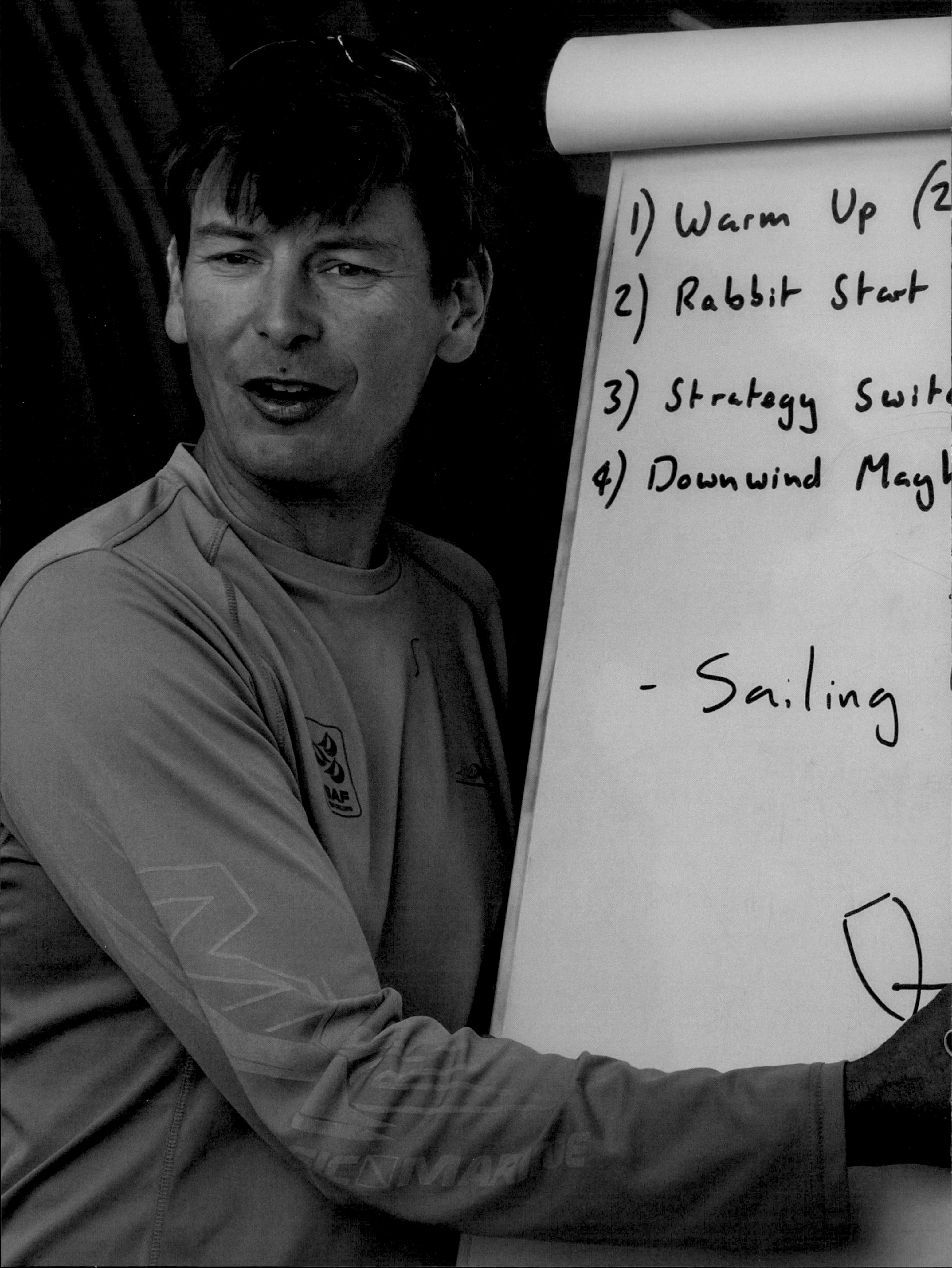

1) Warm Up (2
2) Rabbit Start
3) Strategy Swit
4) Downwind Mayl

- Sailing

One of the strategies encouraged by Cross and Rodrigues at Balatonfüred was gradual improvement by stages. If a sailor reached the weather mark in 10th position, they suggested his or her goal should be to try and pass two or three boats on the downwind leg. Next time, the sailor should try to get to the weather mark in 8th position. The idea was for sailors to set small, reachable goals for themselves all around the race course. Cross and Rodrigues also preached the need to look ahead at the next leg before they rounded the mark: if they had a late wind shift going upwind, they should be thinking about how that shift would affect their choice of course after they rounded the mark and eased the sail. And there were lengthy discussions about a score of details including position in the boat, heel angles, vang tension, centerboard position, sailing by the lee, and the all-important telltales that Cross can't emphasize enough.

"I'm standing there, 50 years old, listening to all this," George Johns says, "and thinking if someone had explained these things to me when I was a kid I wouldn't have stayed in the bottom third of the fleet for so long."

Pedro Rodrigues said the improvement he saw even on a daily basis was scary. "We filmed the same exercises on day one and day five so we could compare how people were sailing," Rodrigues says, "and it was shocking how much everyone improved. It's rewarding as a professor when the kids come to learn from you and work hard to do their best, do the maneuvers, ask the questions. They trusted us. It's great fun to work like that."

One of the creative aspects of teaching is turning situations that occur into learning experiences. That happened with Maria Erdi, an 18- year-old sailor now living in Balatonfüred, who has been something of a phenomenon since she started sailing competitively in 2012. In one of the races during the two-day regatta that wraps up ENP clinics, Erdi was disqualified for Rule 42, the much-discussed rule that says skippers "may adjust the trim of sails and hull…but shall not otherwise move their bodies to propel the boat." Such propulsion is usually rocking, or pumping. Like the calling of balls and strikes in baseball, the infringement of Rule 42 is a judgment by race officials that is always received with displeasure, often outrage. Even though the ENP regatta was small and inconsequential, Maria Erdi was in tears. Her parents were concerned the DSQ would hurt her chances to be selected for the World Cup regatta in Weymouth, a month later. (Erdi would make Weymouth in June 2015, finishing 32nd of 36 boats.)

Cross and Rodrigues stood firm, their assessment being that Erdi was indeed in violation of Rule 42, and for her to experience disqualification would be good for her in the long run. "She is a very good sailor," Rodrigues says. "After the first training day we saw she should win every race. But she did not win every race. The idea was to make it more difficult for her, to measure the reaction of a young girl who has been disqualified, who now has more pressure to win. Because sooner or later she will pass through setbacks in serious regattas. If sailors are good, we have to push more in this school of racing. Otherwise they will not learn from us."

Maria Erdi would go on to take the gold medal in the 2015 Youth Worlds held in Langkawi,

They trusted us. It's great fun to work like that

Tim Cross goes over the basics.

Malaysia, with scores of 3-5-6-1-1-2-(23)-1-4, and no DSQ.

Given the handsome, upscale nature of the Lake Balaton scene, and the fact that Hungary places in the top third of the world's countries in many, diverse international rankings, one has to wonder how the category of "emerging" applies to this small, historically rich nation of ten million people. András Holczhauser says that caused him a bit of a problem when he was organizing the event. "People said to me, `we are not emerging!' But in many cases we are still emerging when it comes to sailing. There is no strong structure behind us. Having Tim Cross and Pedro Rodrigues here was illuminating."

Holczhauser arranged for the two nominated experts to return to Balatonfüred in April 2016, to run training programs that would certify coaches, enabling them to work in all the countries where World Sailing is represented. He is also interacting with the physical education programs of Hungarian universities to include specific training for sailing coaches. "Today's university programs don't really fit sailing because of the sport's special needs," Holczhauser says. "Universities are experts in education, but we are experts in sailing, so we hope to do a joint venture with them in coach development."

Sailing at the youth level is growing in Hungary. In 2013, there were 280 young people sailing. In 2016 the number has risen 20%, to more than 390 youngsters who are sailing Optis, 420s, and 29ers. Hungary's popular summer sports camps are beginning to include sailing.

"The ENP program helps all this grow," Holczhauser says, "helps provide the structure and organization for the coaches and trainers, gives them access to a standardized approach. It helps them not only develop sailors in the best possible way, but also guide them along a path that leads to satisfaction, and maybe even a medal or two."

> "I like that we are sailing two times a day. We also have the theory side. They are filming us a lot. That helps me see things I could not see on the water, and helps me understand what happened out there."
>
> Andrei Zitti, Sailor, Romania

Fitness, an integral part of sailing, is easy to overlook when a proper program (coaching) is not in place. There was no time for the gymnasium at ENP clinics, but the young sailors stretched every day.

Sailors prepare their boats at the Balatonfüred Yacht Club.

66 The Hungarian Yachting Association was founded in 1929 in Balatonfüred. We have 131 clubs as members and approximately 4,000 people who compete and do regattas frequently. Around 30 – 35,000 people sail regularly on Lake Balaton 99

András Holczhauser, General Secretary of the Hungarian Yachting Association

It's doubtful that any of those 4,000 sail more aggressively than the Laser class at the ENP clinic in Balatonfüred.

Estere Kumpina (LAT)

Very little wind and a gorgeous day on Lake
Balatonfüred – what's a sailor to do?

Hungary was one of
the few venues that
produced 29ers, an
increasingly popular
youth class.

> " It's a great opportunity for young sailors to come here because a lot of them have been sailing only at a national level. Here they get a big picture of how sailing looks. If they are youth sailors they'll probably continue into Olympic sailing, so this ENP clinic is a great opportunity for them to improve their performance. For us it's huge. "

Zaklina Lithuaniece, coach, Latvia

There was also a fleet of 420s in Hungary. The coaches conducted drills in tight quarters to focus on boat handling

The Balatonfüred Yacht Club (above) is the latest jewel in this ancient, colorful Hungarian resort town known originally for it's calming natural baths.

Maria Erdi

A day in the life

Maria Erdi started sailing quite by accident. In 2010, her family wanted to move from Budapest into a less urban environment, and decided on Balatonfüered. Maria was 12 years old. None of her family sailed, but suddenly this beautiful lake was in Maria's life. She gave sailing a try, taking lessons after school at Tihany, a small village on a peninsula five miles from her home. She loved being on the lake in summer, and showed such intuitive grasp of sailing that her coach suggested she compete. He put her in a Cadet, a ten-foot, hard-chine pram. "I didn't enjoy the Cadet, or being a crew," Maria says. "I didn't like sailing with someone else."

But the idea of competing on the water wouldn't go away. A year later, at age 14, she looked into a 420, but couldn't find anyone to sail with. "It's hard to find someone who wants it as much as you do," she says. "I asked about singlehanded boats."

First she tried a Byte, an unforgiving 12-foot, 100-pound performance dinghy known for its tendency to capsize. After sailing it less than a year, she won the Byte (CII) gold medal in the 2013 Youth Olympic Class. Then the Laser Radial was suggested, and she fell in love with it. In just a year, she won the 2014 Youth World Championship in the Under 17 (U17) Laser Radial class.

Having been twice selected as Hungary's Youth Sailor of the Year, Maria was in a league of her own at the ENP clinic on Lake Balatonfüred, but she says she still learned plenty. "Every time I sail I learn something," she says. "And having all the coaches there was good because you can learn something different from each one of them. We did some unusual exercises on the water. In one, we were divided into two groups. One group had to tack on headers. The other had to tack on lifts. Most of us know you don't tack on lifts, but it was a memorable demonstration."

Maria credits her success to combining natural talents with hard work and dedication, plus her love of competition. It started at home with the piano. She began playing at age seven, and was soon having two lessons a week. "I really like to win," Maria says. "I have four siblings. They were taking piano too, and I wanted to be better. Playing tennis, I worked hard to beat my two older sisters. Coaches are pushing me always," she says, "but I enjoy it, I never miss a session. It matters a lot that you sail every day."

In 2015, Maria became European Laser Radial Champion, and World Champion at the Laser Radial Worlds (Canada). At the ENP clinic in Balatonfüred, she was selected to attend the Youth Worlds in Malaysia where she capped a brilliant year with a gold medal. Now she's focused on the Olympics. She knows Rio is a long shot for her, but thinks the Tokyo Games (2020) are an attainable goal. "It's getting more and more serious," Maria says. "I'm trying to close the gap now between the youth fleet and the senior fleet, trying to catch up with the best girls. I'm spending more time in the gym, and more time with the psychologist."

She's been signed by Adidas as one of their official athletes. That's a feather in her cap, a prized sponsorship. It also adds pressure. "My contract says they can drop me if I don't continue scoring top results," Maria says, "but I don't think a lot about it."

That resolve should serve her well on the rigorous pathway to the ultimate competition.

The gregarious Erdi with young hopefulls (right). Whether coaching beginners, getting friendly with her sister's horses, playing four hands (mostly classical), or dressed to compete on the water, Maria Erdi always seems to be enjoying herself.

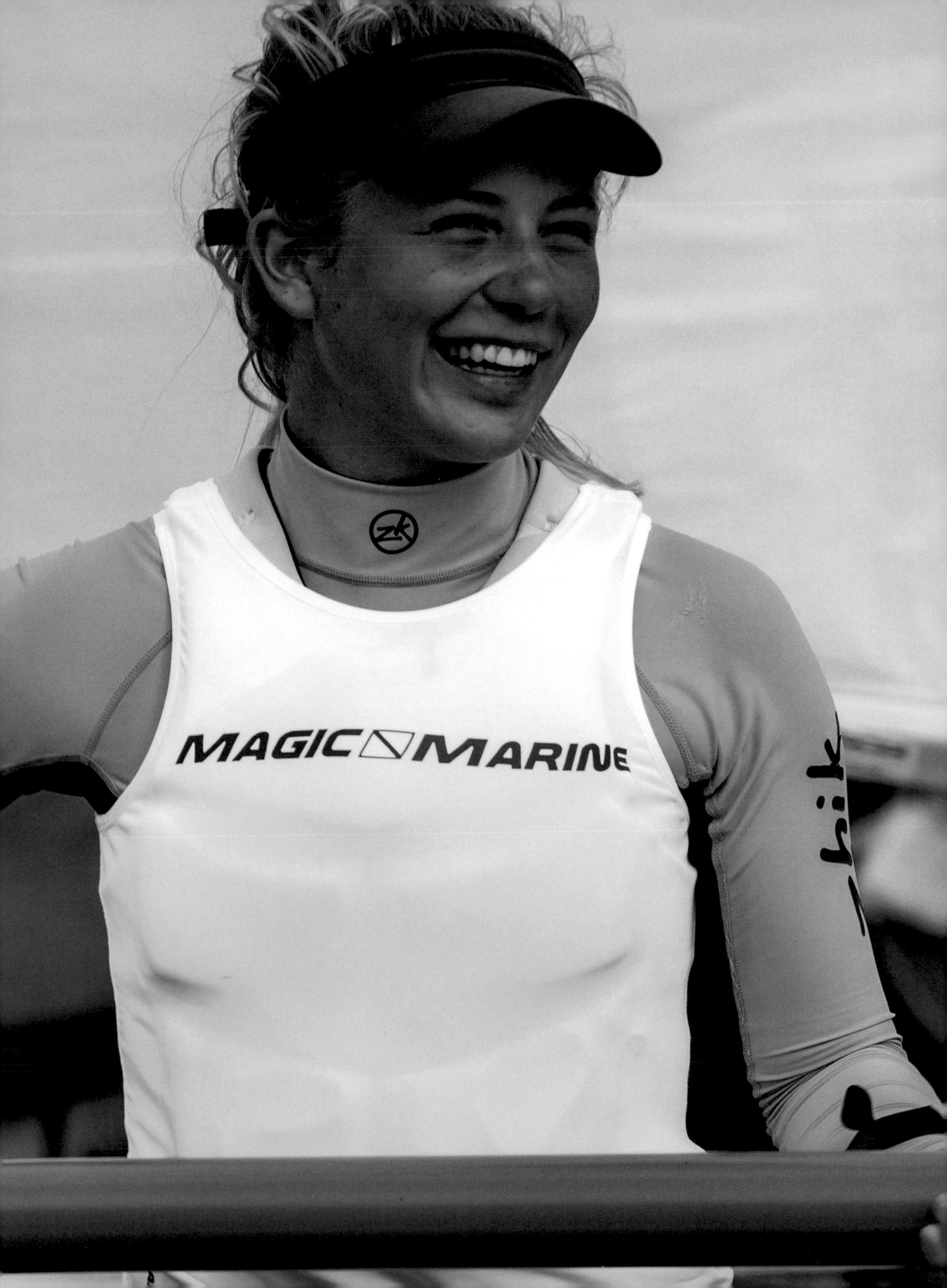
MAGIC MARINE

89

MOZAMBIQUE

Mozambique

Including Tanzania, Angola, Seychelles, Algeria, Tunisia, Sudan, and Egypt

Photographs by Trevor Wilkins

Maputo, the capitol of Mozambique, is a city of one million on Africa's southeast coast. Looking at the foreign-built high-rise apartment buildings along the beach, and the office towers further inland, the aerial view conveys prosperity. The reality is extreme inequality. Mozambique ranks among the poorest and most underdeveloped countries. With a coastline of 1500 miles, it is the 35th largest country in the world – twice the size of California. Urbanization has put pressure on Maputo, where poverty is prevalent. The city's roads are potholed, the buildings poorly maintained. In the slums, rank open pits suffice for sewage facilities. Visitors stroll the lovely beaches at their peril. The catch-22 about the traffic lights is telling about life in Maputo: the lights only work at Christmas, but because Christmas is not celebrated, they don't work then either.

For the Emerging Nations Program held in Maputo, the emphasis was on "emerging." World Sailing's Nominated Experts Rob Holden and Eduardo Sylvestre ran the clinic. "It's a challenge," Holden said, "to convince someone who is not sure where his next meal is coming from that sailing would be a good thing for him to do." For Holden, who hails from Mossel Bay in South Africa, coaching is a passion, his life. He's worked at it for ten years and is currently World Sailing's Regional Development Coordinator for Africa. He knows Maputo, and takes the challenge in stride, because he sees sailing gaining headway and making a difference there. "The world of African kids is three blocks big," Holden says. "To school, to the shop,

and back home. Sailing can open up their world, and that's the dream I have for African children."

One reason sailing is gaining momentum in Maputo is traceable to a handful of old sailors who were involved with the Mozambican Federation of Sailing and Canoeing. These men fought to bring sailing to kids from the street and local neighborhoods. Over many years, they solved the impossibility of kids being able to acquire boats by persuading the local Olympic Committee to provide them. The well-maintained Optis, Lasers, and 420s owned by the Federation are kept at the Clube Maritimo de Desporto, on Maputo Bay. If young people express interest, and show some initiative, they will find themselves on the water. Helio Alberta De Rosa, current president of the Federation, carries on this mission with gusto. "Ninety-nine percent of the kids in Mozambique could not participate if they did not have subsidiary money, or a boat to use," De Rosa says.

Another reason sailing has a niche in Maputo has to do with heritage. Eduardo Sylvestre was amazed to discover the area's traditional fishing fleet of sailing canoes, some 100-strong, that are still working every day. "The fishermen leave early in the morning and sail out miles into the ocean," Sylvestre says. "Their ancestors used to do this. So the kids here have something unique. Sailing is part of their ongoing heritage. Now it's their fathers and grandfathers who are fishing from the sailing canoes. The influence trickles down."

More challenges for Holden and Sylvestre

were provided by the variety of languages and cultures, and a wide disparity of sailing abilities among the sailors and coaches from the other seven countries. "The girl from Sudan was very weak," Holden says. "She was used to sailing on the Nile River once a month in a 26-foot steel boat that weighs a ton and a half. She hadn't had much time in Lasers. Wind on the Nile averages four knots. She had trouble coping with the average of 10 to 12 knots in Maputo. We gave her as much time as we could, but we had to keep in mind this was a performance clinic."

Several coaches from the less developed countries were simply friends or parents of the sailors, adults who had never sailed. "That complicated things tremendously," Holden said. "We had to start somewhere, so we provided them with exercises for the kids, and taught them what a good sail shape and a well-sailed boat looks like."

The predominant languages in Africa are Arabic, French, Portuguese, and English. The experts used the coaches from various countries as translators both on the race course and in the classes. "If you speak English," Holden said, "you can communicate with most people, but them coming back to you is difficult."

One would be hard-pressed to assemble a more troubled group of countries than those represented at the ENP in Mozambique. Collectively, their inadequacies include often severe human and civil rights violations, the presence of active terrorist cells, rampant poverty, the abuse of women and gays, religious persecution, wholesale ivory poaching, and general unrest. Even the lovely Seychelles – 116 islands off the East Coast (population 90,000) that is an idyllic tourist destination – has the highest incarceration rate in the world because of piracy practiced by local criminals.

But the young sailors gathered at Maputo left national problems at home. On the first couple days, there was some polarization based on language and culture. By day three, as photographer Trevor Wilkins expressed it, "It was amazing how they all went through the ice breakers and forged friendships. Teasing between kids using body language was quite remarkable." Wilkins is a native of Cape Town, where he has long worked with young people to develop life skills through sailing. "Three of the countries represented are predominantly Muslim," Wilkins says. "One girl from Sudan wore her scarf all the time to hide her face. When you see a lady sailing her boat in a hijab, you look twice. I have to say she was very gracious about it, while her father looked quite concerned. In some countries a Muslim woman might be treated as second class. Not here."

"They all bonded," Eduardo Sylvestre says. "The Christian girls all talked to the Sudanese girl, asking her questions about the hijab, and she loosened up, got more comfortable. One afternoon after sailing

National problems were left at home

we saw her and three other girls walking down the beach, all holding hands. It was a fantastic sight. If it weren't for sailing, it never would have happened."

For Sylvestre, the highlight of the event was when he coached the girl from Angola for a day after her coach was taken ill. "She was in the top ten," Eduardo said. "Then she committed a foul and had to do a penalty turn. She was devastated, in tears. I asked why she was crying, told her to just say goodbye to that mistake. I told her she had to turn it over, focus on the next race and what she had to do. The next day she got a first and a second. She thanked me, said she had learned to put mistakes behind her and move on."

Clube Maritimo was built by the Mozambique Olympic Committee. It has been put to good use by the Federation. Their sailing team frequently wins the African sailing championship. Their canoe teams are world class. The Clube provided a good

Sailing with a hijab (head scarf) is de rigueur for a Muslim girl from Sudan.

classroom for the morning sessions, while the broad bay, open to the prevailing easterly winds, proved to be an excellent place to sail. Sylvestre says there were half a dozen very good sailors in the group, all eager to learn. Chief among them was Andre Felipe, from Angola. "Andre is quiet, observant," Sylvestre says. "He listens, pays attention, asks questions. I got to follow him because I was also coach at the Youth Worlds. Filipe was consistently sailing almost a lap ahead of everyone in Maputo, winning every race. But at the Worlds he finished 40th. There is a gap, for sure. But because of what we are doing, the gap is getting smaller."

Part of the problem that needs to be addressed is follow-up in the various countries. In the six months since the clinic, Andre Felipe had sailed only four times. It was the same with the Egyptian sailor, Elmerdash Ali Moutaz. He had trouble getting boats to sail through his federation. "That's what happens when you don't have a sailing program in the country that supports these kids," Sylvestre says. "It's a good thing World Sailing is running these ENPs. If they didn't do it, it would be a huge problem because the gap would get ever bigger and they'd never close it."

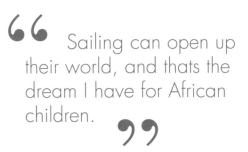

Rob Holden, Nominated Expert
(World Sailing)

"
Having experience with other coaches allows us to discuss things we learn in the classroom and put theory into practice in a practical way.

At Clube Maritime Sports we work with kids who don't have much money. We start them swimming at the club, then they have the opportunity to sail and grow up with the Clube. "

Cesar Sanchez , Coach, Mozambique

At low tide, a sand bar provided just another obstacle for sailors in Maputo.

The Mozambican Federation of Sailing and Canoeing ran the clinic, providing boats, gear, and good food for the sailors.

66 I will remember the exercises and the lessons. I will remember the hospitality of the Mozambican people, and the regattas. They gave us the equipment and they gave us the time and the money to have this clinic 99

Azzam Gaffhr Elhssam, coach, Sudan

66 This week was very, very strange because I've never been in something like this. We all learned many things that sailors have to work on. It was good to share the experience with other countries. Most of all we enjoyed and gave something back to each other. It was a good week 99

Adriano Candido, coach, Mozambique

66 World Sailing people are very
professional. They have all the knowledge
and they have all the patience to handle
the commotion. This will definitely lift up
the level of sailors in Africa and I hope
that they do it quite often because it really
helps and besides, it's fun. 99

Azzam Gaffhr Elhssam, coach, Sudan

I hope they do this quite often because it helps with the sailing, and besides, it's fun. The youth get together and the cultures mix. It's very good.

Azzam Gaffar Elhssam, Coach, Sudan

Coach Antonio Gois, in green and black shirt (at left), huddles with his 420 sailors

> " Sailing opens horizons for the poor, it's a way for young kids to get out of Africa and see new horizons. "

Rob Holden, Nominated Expert

The fishermen of Mozambique (above) carry on under sail , a long tradition that
is beginning to have a positive influence on young sailors. Among their catch is
the blue crab (right). The working waterfront in Maputo is always busy.

Maria Mabjaia
A Day in the Life

In 2014, when she was 16 years old, Maria Mabjaia raced an Optimist dinghy at the All-Africa Games and brought home a bronze medal. Overnight, she became something of an icon in Maputo. Her image was suddenly on posters. A well-known brand named a cookie after her. Her accomplishment reinforced the goal of the Mozambican Sailing and Canoeing Federation to make sailing available to street kids from poor neighborhoods, and helped persuade the local Olympic Committee to purchase more boats.

Maria began sailing when representatives from Clube Maritimo visited her elementary school and asked if any children were interested. "Most of the kids wanted to know, what is sailing?" Maria recalls. She's not sure why, but she decided to try it. To sail, she had to wake up at 3:00 am to catch the only train from her very poor neighborhood to the Clube. When she began to show promise as a sailor, the Clube and the Ministry of Education arranged for her family to move to an area in Maputo close to the Clube.

While the new location is more convenient, the living conditions remain very spare in Maria's small, cement-block dwelling. Photographer Trevor Wilkins, who spent a day with Maria, was attracted to a nearby house in her neighborhood because of more than 20 pair of sandals hanging outside next to some threadbare wetsuits drying in the sun. "Inside was a scene of abject poverty," Wilkins says, "Mattresses on the floor, and stuffing oozing out of couches. Must have been 30 kids sitting on the floor, all sailors, kids who are out there performing without much support."

Wilkins has covered many high-end events in his career, including the Volvo and Cape Town/Rio ocean races. But he said this shoot for him was "awe-inspiring, about touching the inner core of young people. We were standing in the cleanly raked yard of Maria's house," Wilkins says, "and her mother came out holding a beautiful sarong in both hands. She presented it to my assistant, Ashleigh. Now that sarong would cost about 300 rand ($20 US) back home, a lot of money for Maria's mom. You can bet we shed a tear or three. But these people are givers, never asking what have you got for us."

Mrs. Mabjaia hopes her daughter keeps training. "Sometimes her friends think it's too risky," she says. "They wonder if Maria will die in the sea."

"They tell me I'm a fish," Maria says with a smile.

"I'm very proud of her," her mother says. "I agreed to her sailing to help with her shyness. She wouldn't play with the others, wouldn't have any fun. But I never thought I would get to see her like this. She is having fun, doing real things, and is recognized. I hope she keeps training and gets much, much better and dedicates herself to the sport God gave her. It's my dream to keep her sailing."

❝ To get to Tokyo 2020 is not easy, but it's not difficult either. You just need to be dedicated to what you want. That's it. You need to be very dedicated, to know what you want and what you are going to do there and why you are doing it. That's why I'm so motivated. ❞

Maria Mabjaia (MOZ)

Maria and her contemporaries (upper left) teach youngsters English as well as sailing. Maria with her mother (left), whose name is also Maria, and her sisters. Mother Maria breaks into a dance outside her home in Maputo (above). The young Maria's notoriety has resulted in her own brand of biscuits.

“ Everywhere you looked there was sailing kit on the walls. They're very poor and it must have been worth a lot of money but no-one was worried. There's such a community and the young sailors are such a big part of that. Sailing gives the whole village hope for the future, everyone we spoke to said the same thing: every success these kids have is a success for everyone. ”

Dan Haggett, Official Videographer

ANTIGUA

SPORTS CENTRE

Antigua and Barbuda

Including British Virgin Islands, Turks and Caicos, Barbados, Guatemala,
Cayman Islands, Trinidad and Tobago, Belize, Uruguay, U.S. Virgin Islands, Ecuador

Photographs by Daniel Forster

During the last race of the two-day regatta that wrapped up the ENP clinic in Antigua, it was blowing 20 knots with higher gusts. It was hard work sailing the Laser Radials upwind for the 17 young skippers in attendance. Downwind the boats were on a tear, flinging thick walls of spray to the wind, providing a pulse-pounding challenge for the soaking-wet skippers to keep their boats upright and on track.

One of the last boats to cross the finish line was skippered by Blanca Velasquez from Belize, at age 13 the youngest sailor in the fleet. Blanca surfed her Laser across the line, eased the sheet and let the boat round up and stop, sail luffing madly. Then she dramatically collapsed into the cockpit and rolled onto her back motionless, arms outstretched, as if she had expired. Blanca's comical pratfall got a lot of laughs from the crowd of skippers and officials around the finish line, because everyone could relate. The last race had provided a fitting conclusion to an intense week of training.

The ENP clinic in Antigua began taking shape in late 2000, when Elizabeth Jordan received a letter from Dan Jaspers at ISAF, saying he was looking into Antigua as a place for developing youth sailing. Antigua, the principal island of Antigua and Barbuda, consists of only 108 square miles. It is a green, hilly island in the heart of the Caribbean with sun-drenched beaches, population 90,000. It thrives on tourism. One of Jaspers' first exploratory letters went to Jordan because Antigua is also a well-known center for winter sailing, and Elizabeth happened to be Commodore of the Antigua Yacht Club at the time.

A fit, attractive blonde in her 60s with boundless energy, a talent for organization, and an irresistibly straightforward way of getting things done, Elizabeth Jordan had arrived in English Harbor by boat six months before. Deciding she'd had enough of her medical-research business in the UK, she and three other women had sailed her Swan 36 transatlantic, then made for Antigua's annual Race Week.

She never left. She chartered out of English Harbor for two and a half years, says it was the hardest job she ever had – sailing, cleaning, cooking and entertaining full-time while living on her boat. The Antigua Yacht Club spotted her as a live one and kept reelecting her as their commodore for six years. "People do less time for murder," Elizabeth says quietly in crisp, British intonation, keeping a poker face. While commodore, she started her National Sailing Academy where young Antiguans can learn to swim and sail free of charge.

"There was no outreach for local kids," Elizabeth says. "Most of the kids sailing were children of expatriates. I wanted to do something for the locals. I asked the government, why isn't sailing a national sport here? You can't be more than six miles from water anywhere on this island.

Unfortunately the legacy of slavery left a fear of the water among West Indians. We had to get over that cultural hurdle. But now it's happening. The new generations are okay."

The government was so relieved Elizabeth wasn't asking for money they granted her use of the national coat of arms for her logo, and agreed

The captains welcomed her on board

to verbally support her efforts. She went to the visiting yachts for money. Every year from October to March, English Harbor's expansive network of concrete docks is full to capacity with boats of all sizes – predominately super maxis -- from around the world. Being commodore of the local yacht club gave Elizabeth carte blanch to roam the docks and visit the yachts. The captains all welcomed her aboard for a drink, at which point she would collect for the Sailing Academy. "When they saw the little kids in the sailboats they got the picture," Elizabeth says. "I asked them all to give me one US dollar per foot of their length." Many did that, and more. It's difficult to say no to Elizabeth Jordan.

As luck would have it, Jordan struck a deal for a piece of property on English Harbor just in time for the Emerging Nations Program event. The property had failed several times as a restaurant, meaning there was a large room with a bar that could double as dining room and classroom. There was also a natural launching ramp, and by the time the ENP event started, a handsome 180-foot dock had been financed and built. When the sailors and coaches from ten other countries descended upon Antigua in July 2014, the National Sailing Academy had been officially open for just five months. In that time, Elizabeth had built and rented a dive shop, spruced up an attractive rental cottage on the

Elizabeth Jordan, Founder of the
National Sailing Academy.

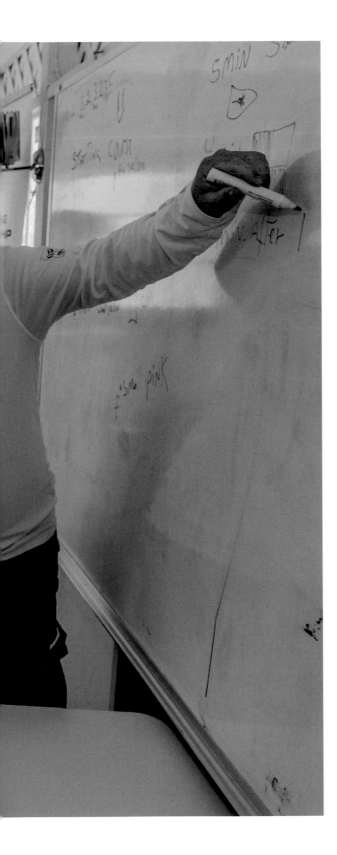

property, assembled the required number of boats and gear, and found volunteers to help her cook and serve three meals a day for a week.

Having fine-tuned their approach to ENP events in previous venues, Nominated World Sailing Experts Tim Cross and Eduardo Sylvestre got things rolling with a brief classroom session that outlined the week's activities. Then it was feet wet.

I asked them for one US dollar per foot

"You never quite know what you're going to get when you start the clinic," Tim Cross said. "You never know the real quality of the sailors or of the coaches, so you adapt the core syllabus, tweak the delivery to maximize the benefits to the needs of the people who are here. The coaches are a very important part of the clinic. They must be as interactive as possible, not take a back seat. We brief the coaches and get feedback from them so they will move into leading some of the training sessions out on the water. Then we ensure that their follow-up with their sailors has good value."

Coaches are destined to play a big role in the growth of developing nations' sailing programs. Both Cross and Sylvestre are designated World Sailing "mentors," which means they strive to involve emerging nations in World Sailing programs. Having those nations buy into coaching standards is high on the list. "We have to show them we have a structure, we have a program," Sylvestre says, "and there are opportunities, with scholarships, where they can go to learn coaching and progress through the various levels – where they can be taught how to do it, what to expect, how to start a sailing school, how to keep the kids interested after they age out of Optis.

"Each country is different," Sylvestre says. "Here, Elizabeth goes to the schools and says okay, we have a program. They come here, they don't have

World Sailing Nominated Expert Eduardo Silvestre addresses situations in the classroom that will later be practised on the water

to pay. If there was no program like this the kids would be playing soccer or basketball, I don't know what, but it wouldn't be sailing."

On the water, Cross and Sylvestre split the group in half for various drills including starts, mark roundings, sailing downwind (tactics, trimming for speed), general boat handling (tacks, jibes, capsize drills), and tactical situations.

They talked about strategic risk

The classroom sessions were lively, thanks to video shot by Cross and Sylvestre during the drills that was shown on a big-screen TV borrowed from Elizabeth. While Cross admonished his charges for being constantly over early on starts, he liked the fact that they were so competitive. Sylvestre emphasized having clear air at the start, and talked about when being in the second row at the favored end made sense. They asked skippers who had done well to talk about their strategies. They talked about strategic risk on the race course.

Eduardo said many skippers were too worried about the traffic at the start when they should be looking ahead at wind pressure and direction – at what would be happening in 30 seconds. They spent a lot of time on pumping (complex Rule 42, about when rocking the boat is legal), and on posture: "Good posture in the boat helps support your weight," Cross said. "When you slouch, it makes your body heavy, causes the boat to sink." Sylvestre emphasized fitness, the need to regularly attend a proper gym. Cross kept harping on watching tell tales, "because they tell the truth!"

The kids got to see both their mistakes and their cool moves on the video, which led to a lively exchange of friendly banter. By the second day, it was as if this ad hoc, multi-national group of young sailors had been together for years. One could see friendships developing. Most of the kids came from three- to five-boat fleets, so they were thrilled to be among 17 boats on the starting line. But mainly, they were learning why "away games" are so important to racing sailboats: they were watching one another like hawks, picking up useful ideas and techniques, from new ways to rig their boats to different sailing techniques.

"One morning I was discussing weight positioning in a heavy breeze with Mathias Dyck, from Ecuador," 17-year-old Antiguan sailor Jules Mitchell said. "He told me if you sit further aft you have more control of your steering."

"There's always something to learn when you sail with new people," said Florence Allan, a 17-year-old from the Cayman Islands, "no matter what their skill level is." Allan has learned a lot in her short career. Six months after the clinic she was invited by the Cayman Islands Olympic Committee to compete in the Rio Games. She had Tokyo (2020) in mind, never dreamed she would make Rio. "I'm still taking it in," Allan said. "It feels surreal."

It's the nature of any racing fleet to divide itself more or less in half, and the ENP fleet in Antigua was no exception. Age was the defining factor, with the older, more experienced sailors consistently in the front. Mathias Dyck was dominant. A serious 18-year-old without an ounce of fat on his gym-friendly body, Dyck learned to sail on a lake in the mountains of San Pablo, Ecuador, thanks to his family's participation in the sport, and their support. He was perhaps the only sailor in the group who had been to several Opti world and national

Good sailing begins with proper rigging ashore.

championships.

The struggle for second through fifth was no more hard fought than the competition for 14th through 16th. And one of the better sailors got everyone's attention when he decided to quit during the last race after realizing that finishing first was mathematically impossible. His coach took him to task. For both him, and the rest of the fleet, his behavior was a useful learning experience.

World Sailing has announced the ENP has a five-year life span. "I hope it goes on for 20 years," Eduardo Sylvestre said. "If we want better sailors, there is no better way than having a clinic like this. We want all these sailors to know each other, keep competing and improving because sailing is not just for championships -- sailing is a lifetime thing."

Chet Green, Minister of Sport for Antigua and Barbuda, agrees. Green stopped by the National Sailing Academy on the final day to put his country's official stamp of approval on the proceedings. The sport of cricket rules in Antigua, with the best batsman in the world , Vivian Richards, a member of its national team. Minister Green used Richard's predominance as an example he hoped sailors from Antigua will follow. "Just as we are known for cricket," Green said, "we want to be known for sailing. We pledge to the National Sailing Academy and World Sailing the government's full, all-out support to this program and its success. The program is in its infancy, but in four or five years, we'll be beating the world."

> " The big message here is how to perform to a high standard on the race course "
>
> Tim Cross (GBR)
> Nominated Expert

Tim Cross brings his coach boat in close to critique the style of a sailor.

They were long days on and off the water. Given only a week, the sailors focussed, soaking up as much knowledge and information as possible.

Having room
at the leeward
mark is always
cause for a
smile.

Not a drill: Jalese Gordon (ANT), age 13, capsized in 20 knots during the regatta in Antigua. She struggled long and hard to get up and running again, and perservered.

Antigua provided reliably strong winds that consistently challenged the 30 young skippers. Experts Tim Cross and Eduardo Sylvestre were impressed by how well most of the sailors from the 10 countries represented at the clinic handled the conditions.

Cameraman Mike Audick [at left] documented the Laser jam at the launching ramp at days end. Boats were washed down and put away with care.

Antigua is relaxed, colorful
like its lizards, a small island
of many faces. A sailor
relaxes, and a steel band
rocks atop Shirley Heights
as the sun sets on Freeman's
Bay and English Harbor,
where Admiral Nelson once
careened his ships

Jules Mitchell &
Rhone Kirby

A Day in the Life

For two Antiguan skippers, a lot was riding on the fourth and final race of the two day regatta that capped the ENP clinic at English Harbor.

Jules Mitchell [below right], age 16, was leading Rhone Kirby [below left], age 17, by three points after two races. Kirby rallied to beat Mitchell by three boats in race three, making them all-even going into the last race. Only one of them could be selected to go to the Youth World Championships in Malaysia in December. Race four was for all the marbles. To add more tension to the situation, the two are good friends.

Both had good starts in race four, but Mitchell picked up a little shift on the right going to the first weather mark, and despite Kirby's best efforts, Mitchell held off his friend to the

finish. Kirby finished a couple boat lengths behind Mitchell, a matter of a few seconds in the planing conditions.

Ashore, after the race, Rhone Kirby was distraught. For a few minutes he sat with a friend, his face shrouded in disappointment. Then, showing remarkable poise for a boy his age, he straightened his shoulders, congratulated his friend Jules, and talked about his loss. "Jules is a bit bigger than me," Kirby said. "I know I'm a bit smarter than him in the head, but he's smarter physically. In the bigger winds he's faster than me. I was surprised I overpowered him in today's first race, but he can hike better, and it's a big competition between the two of us. I just blew it, lost to him by one point."

Jules Mitchell also handled himself well. He said in the last race he had intended to match race Rhone, and in fact had him pinned during the last ten seconds before the start. But he could not follow through by pushing him over the line early. "I couldn't do that to a friend," Jules said.

The next day, the two boys spent the day visiting old haunts, and, of course, sailing.

These two pals love to compete, whether it's sailing the academy's 1720, leaping for mangoes, or running at Jolly Harbor, where Jules learned to sail. Rhone learned at the Antigua Yacht Club's Sailing Centre (top). The boys compare gear and trophies at Jules's house (page opposite, upper left) and Rhone's (upper right). Jules' mother, Susan Athilll, provided the pancakes, and the dogs.

PFDs dry in the Antiguan sun at the National Sailing Centre.

MALAYSIA

Malaysia

Including Including Vietnam, Pakistan, and Chinese Taipai

Photographs by Christophe Launay

Even paradise has its bad moments.

Langkawi, Malaysia, where an ENP clinic was held in October 2015, is widely considered one of the prettiest, most environmentally congenial spots on earth. By some rankings it is one of the top two places in the world to retire. But when Tim Cross, who would co-run the clinic with fellow Nominated Expert Pedro Rodrigues, went to board his connecting flight from Kuala Lumpur to the island, he discovered all flights had been canceled for at least 24 hours.

It seemed that Langkawi was buried in a thick cloud of smoke that had blown in from neighboring Indonesia on the southeasterly breeze. Cross had run smack into a contentious program in the area called "slash and burn": devastating forest fires lit in the name of "landscape manipulation" for plantation development. Palm oil in particular. It's a heated, international environmental and health issue, with a variety of practitioners ranging from big corporations to small farmers pointing fingers at one another.

Once in Langkawi, Cross found plenty of Lasers and 420s on hand for the clinic. The boats were being assembled for the Youth World Championships that would be held in Langkawi in December 2015. But where was the water? The "super" moon was closest to the earth in October,

creating unusual, extreme tides. Sailors would be up to their knees in mud getting to the slipway. And where was the wind? It rained every morning for three days, a condition locals knew foretold very light, very fickle wind in the afternoon. "I have to admit," Cross says, "it had us scratching our heads. We wondered how the Worlds could possibly be held here. It was challenging. Then it cleared, we finally saw the other side of the harbor, the breeze filled in, and we got to appreciate what great sailing this location can offer."

Mohd Afendy Abdullah, who is general manager of the Malaysian Sailing Association, says he fell in love with what Langkawi could offer in 2000, when he first set foot on the island. "I took one look at this place and said we should start something here," Afendy says. He began by organizing a small sailing team. "From there, I started working on the government, asking for funding and a small piece of land to develop a facility." Afendy says he studied the wind patterns, and discovered a tunnel effect right across the inner harbor. "The wind was always stronger here than any place in Malaysia," Afendy says. "That's how we convinced the government to build the National Sailing Center in this place."

The smoke having dissipated, Cross and Rodrigues focused on how to present the clinic. "The syllabus is always the same," Rodrigues says,

The 40-foot statue in Langkawi's Eagle Square (Datarn Lang) harks to the island's name in colloquial Malay: island of the reddish brown eagle.

"but it had to be a very different approach from the other venues because the participants were very different." The perplexing babble of Pakistani, Vietnamese, Chinese, and Malaysian languages created an initial stumbling block. "We used some of the sailors, who were good in English, to help us," Rodrigues says. "We never knew at the end of the day what information was lost in translation, but that's all we could do." During the classroom sessions, Tim and Pedro found themselves speaking slowly, then waiting until brief explanations between sailors using hand gestures and body language were completed before continuing.

As usual, video was shot on the water, then played back in classroom sessions to demonstrate both mistakes and proper sailing. Words are a small part of that technique. As for tuning, the 420 coaches were out there raking the masts with a gage. Everyone can understand numbers.

Add to the language problems the varied mix of cultures and religion, and it wasn't possible for the group of sailors to coalesce into a unified cohort. But it also wasn't a problem. "The kids understood their differences," Rodrigues says. "They all understood and respected those differences, and we did as well."

Tim and Pedro's approach was to concentrate on the basics prior to moving into more performance-oriented elements: proper rigging and preparation of the boats, and making sure the essentials of sailing – body position on all points of sail, sail trim, and the school moves of tacking and jibing – were performed by the book. "A place like Hungary was all about performance,"

Rodrigues says, "but in Langkawi there was no sailor in the group who could lead the others by example."

The Malaysians taught them to sail

The Emerging Nations Program was designed to improve the performance of capable sailors. Cross and Rodrigues were initially stymied when they discovered the delegation of young people from Vietnam simply did not know how to sail. "There was a case for us saying to them, `There has been a misunderstanding. This is not for you, bye bye,'" Rodrigues says. "Teaching sailing is not the aim of these clinics. But we did not feel right excluding them."

Rodrigues says the young sailors from the host country stepped up to welcome the Vietnamese kids to the sport. They suggested engaging them as crews on the 420s, and that's what happened. "They worked every day on the water, sailing," Rodrigues says, with amazement still lingering in his voice. "The Malaysian sailors who sailed with them, they are the ones who taught them to sail. The language problem was intense, but they managed to show them when to push this, move that, pull this line… kids have a facility for communicating that works through different languages. The Vietnamese learned to sail in a week. It was something to see, and very selfless of the Malaysian sailors. If they had been focused on just improving themselves, the Vietnamese would have been relegated to watching

What the well-prepared sailor wears for an afternoon in the Malaysian sun.

from the coach boats, and you don't learn that way. The attitude of the Malaysian sailors, and the ability of the coaches to adapt the clinic so no one would be excluded, was very positive."

For Mohd Afendy Abdullah, having the ENP in Langkawi was another big step in his ongoing dream: to have many Malaysian sailors involved in the Olympics. "We have to make sailing the number-one sport in Malaysia," Affendi says. "Right now, in terms of medals, our sport is number two. We hope in the future sailing will be known as the best sport in Malaysia."

Another step in Afendy's dream would happen in December 2015, when the Youth World Championships would be held in Langkawi.

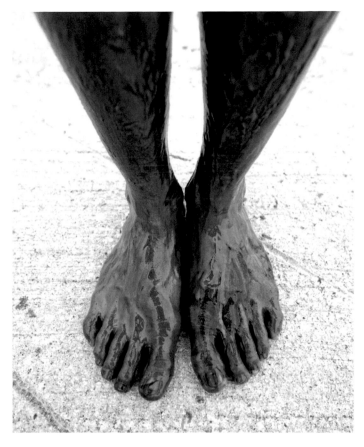

A so-called "super moon", a focal point in the 18 year lunar cycle, created extreme tides during the clinic, causing sailors to slog through knee-deep mud to get boats to the slipway. There was plenty of water from the hose for washing off [page opposite].

Nominated expert Pedro Rodrigues (top and above) creates a situation for the sailors to ponder on the magnet board. Visual aids helped circumvent the language barrier.

Above, 420 sailors go over the intricate layout of the demanding performance dinghy.

> " For me sailing with other sailors from other countries is very good. Being able to sail with other countries has made all our confidence grow. "
>
> Muhammad Uzair (PAK), sailor

With the ENP Clinic and the Youth Worlds taking place in Langkawi just a month apart, boat preparation and maintenance was a priority [page opposite].

167

Young attendees from Vietnam who did not know how to sail were thrown in at the deep end - hooked up on the trapeze by Malaysian skippers. They learned quickly

A Vietnamese participant in the clinic [right] seems pleased at the prospect of racing sailboats while his Malaysian skipper ponders how to proceed.

Four different body positions result in remarkably similar sail trim and heel angle downwind in the Laser Radial fleet, a good subject for classroom discussion in the morning when the video from the previous day was shown.

Pedro Rodrigues who worked with the 420 fleet, was amazed by the success of the Malaysian sailors with the Vietnamese. "They managed to show them when to pull this, push that," he said "Kids have a facility for communicating that works through different languages."

Given its benign weather and friendly attitude, Langkawi is rated as one of the best places in the world to retire. Tour boats with personality (Left) offer sunset cruises. The local fast food is is tasty, and the coconuts plentiful.

SENARAI HARGA

GORENG PISANG	7 KPG RM 1.00	MEE KARI	1 BGKS RM 2.00		
GORENG UBI	5 KPG RM 1.00	NASI LEMAK	1 BGKS RM 1.00	MINUMAN BERPERISA	
GORENG CEMPEDAK	3/4 BIJI RM 1.00	BILIS TELOR	1 BGKS RM 1.00	1 CUP RM .0	
GORENG SUKUN	KPG RM .0	SAMBAL AYAM	1 BGKS RM 1.00	MINUMAN BERKABONAT	
KUIH MUIH	8 BIJI RM1.00	BIHUN SUP	1 BGKS RM 1.50	1 CUP RM L.0	
LAKSA	1 BGKS RM 1.50	BIHUN GORENG	1 BGKS RM 0. 0	Layan	SELF
MEE REBUS	1 BGKS RM .50	KOEY TEAW	1 BGKS RM 0. 0	Diri	SERVICE
CUCUR UDANG	1 BGKS RM 1.00	BUBUR KACANG	1 BGKS RM 2.00		
PASEMBUR	1 BGKS RM 1.00	BUBUR B.PULUT HITAM	1 BGKS RM 2.00		

KHS 6616 KHS 6616

Khairun Hanna Mohd Afendi

A Day in the Life

When you are the fifth oldest of eleven children, and you live on an attractive island, and your siblings are all accomplished sailors, chances are you will learn to sail. It may be difficult at first, but then siblings can be troublesome in such large numbers. Khairun Hanna says she first went sailing with one of her brothers. "He took me out in his Opti," she says, "and made me cry."

Undeterred, she was soon sailing her own Opti. Her father, Mohd Afendy Abdullah, a windsurfer and Malaysian team manager for six years, coached Hanna and the rest of his children in sailing and all other sports. But despite being blessed with a natural feel for sailing a boat, she didn't do very well. "I was too fat," Hanna says with a delightful laugh. At age 12, she switched to the Laser 4.7 and found the larger boat more suited to her physique. She became fit running on her school's track team in the 400 meter and 4x4 relay events. She attended one Youth World Championship in the 4.7, finishing mid-fleet.

Hanna sailed a 420 at the ENP clinic, which she saw as most helpful to the visiting countries that don't sail as much as the Malaysians. "The sailors from Chinese Taipei were quite good," she says. "I never heard of sailors from Pakistan, but they could sail, and they were very funny. They liked to disturb people, make crazy jokes. And we got the Vietnamese kids, who were non-sailors, into the 420s, put them on the trapeze. It was amusing how they got themselves out there at first, but after a few times they were fine. At the end of the program they could sail. There was a language problem, but we all understood each other. It was amazing."

Hanna's English is good. She says her father encouraged her to speak Malay, and she does. But in her final exams she got an A in English, and a B in Malay. That's a good thing, because in her school, all subjects are taught in English.

A member of the national sailing team, Hanna is currently training with a professional coach and a new crew in a 470, with her eye on the Tokyo Olympics in 2020. Her older sister was meant to crew for her, but landed a flight attendant job that forced her to retire from racing. She has another talented sister, Khairunneeta Binte, who won a gold medal in the Southeast Asia Games in 2015 (Laser Radial Team Racing), but she is unavailable.

Hanna's brother, Khairulnizam, the very one who made her cry on her first sail, helps coach her. Khairulnizam represented Malaysia in Lasers in the London Olympics (2012), won a silver medal (Laser) at the 2015 Southeast Asia Games, and is currently in training for Rio. "Khairun is my sailing hero because he qualified for the Olympics at such a young age," Hanna says. "I feel so happy for him, and I want to be just like him." A weekly series of regattas is on Hanna's schedule as a way of pinpointing areas she needs to improve.

179

She finished second in the final ENP regatta in Langkawi. "The Malaysian boys were first," she says. "It's difficult to beat them." At the 2015 Youth Worlds, Hanna finished 16th in the 420 class.

"I'm really proud of my daughter Hanna," Mohd Afendy Abdullah says. "She is a brilliant kid, doing really well with her education as well as sailing. And she always says she wants to go sailing. I want her to go to the Olympics, and hearing that from her makes me very happy."

A ceramic tiger protects Hanna's home in Langkawi [top left]. She sits with her father and youngest brother (Olympic hopeful 2026?), and enjoys dinner with a a few of her ten brothers and sisters.

F YOUTH SAILING
LD CHAMPIONS
NG NATIONS

Youth Sailing World Championships 2015

Langkawi Malaysia

The 45th Youth Worlds held in 2015 were the largest and most successful ever, with 425 sailors from 76 countries competing for the coveted medals in nine different classes. The regatta was a great success.

Unlike the ENP clinic in Langkawi a month before, the wind was mostly reliable at 20 knots, providing great sailing for the competitors. Only on the last day did it become light and variable.

The ENP clinics were well-represented at the Worlds, with 36 sailors taking advantage of World Sailing scholarships. Hungary's Maria Erdi led that group with not only a gold medal in the Laser Radial class, but as winner of the Bengt Julian Trophy. The Julian recipient is selected by fellow youth sailors for having displayed acts of sportsmanship, respect, graciousness, friendliness, and endeavor.

Speaking at the Mahsuri International Exhibition Center in Langkawi, World Sailing Vice President Quanhai Li's remarks celebrated the week-long event. "It is obvious you have enjoyed yourselves and made some new friends," Li told the sailors. "Above all else it has been a pleasure to watch such camaraderie and good manners. You have demonstrated outstanding skills and sportsmanship, but above all a passion for the sport of sailing."

Camaraderie, manners, and a passion for sailing. Does it get any better?

Another stunning Langkawi sunset is reflected in the harbor.

The welcome mat for the 425 sailors was large, and elaborate, including a troupe of local dancers that performed at the opening ceremony. Langkawi's long, careful preparation for the event was evident everywhere. Group selfies [right] were the order of the day.

> " The North East Monsoon wind has just started. The wind will get stronger, and at the Youth Worlds we expect between 15 and 20 knots every day. Everybody will really enjoy it. "

Mohd Afendy Abdullah, General Manager, Malaysian Sailing Association

> " It was really tricky today. I was worried because I had a bad race yesterday, but I got a good start and could control the fleet. "

Maria Erdi (HUN), Gold medalist, Laser Radial (W)

29er

"

As we rounded the gate we were in front, but we knew we had to be four places ahead. Luckily we caught some shifts and finished in front "

Peter Lin Janezic (SLO), 29er (M)

> **“** I feel so happy…it's always unbelievable. It's great to finish my youth career in such a good place with such good people around, and to win is even better **”**

Stefania Elfutina (RUS)
Gold medalist, RS:X (W)

> We were celebrating, then we found out we had a protest. But it all got sorted – we are good friends with the team that protested – and it was such a relief

Will Logue (USA), Gold medalist, 420 (M)

199

Many of the sailors from 76 countries gather for a portrait with boats and flags flying [above].

Bengt Julian trophy winner and Laser Radial gold medalist Maria Erdi stands with Sailing World Cup Manager Antonio Gonzales de la Madrid (far left), former Rolex Sailor of the Year Cory Sertl, Chairman of the Youth Worlds, and (at right), Mohd Afendy Abdullah, General Manager of the Malaysian Sailing Association.

The final dinner and closing ceremonies were held in the handsome dining room of the Mahsuri International Exhibition Center [page opposite]

Appendix

ISAF YOUTH SAILING WORLD CHAMPIONSHIP
LANGKAWI MALAYSIA 2015

HU

Christophe Launay

Appendix A

Youth Sailing World Championships Medalists 2015

Boy's One Person Dinghy - Laser Radial

1	ALISTAIR YOUNG	AUS
2	GEORGE GAUTREY	NZL
3	DANIEL WHITELY	GBR

Boy's Two Person Dinghy - 420

1	WILL LOGUE & BRAM BRAKMAN	USA
2	LEONARDO LOMBARDI & RODRIGO LUZ	BRA
3	DOUGLAS ELMES & COLIN O'SULLIVAN	IRL

Boy's Windsurfer - RS:X

1	TITOUAN LE BOSQ	FRA
2	FRANCISCO SAUBIDET BIRKNER	ARG
3	BRENNO FRANCIOLI	BRA

Girl's One Person Dinghy - Laser Radial

1	MARIA ERDI	HUN
2	HANNAH ANDERSSOHN	GER
3	MAGDALENA KWASNA	POL

Girl's Two Person Dinghy - 420

1	JULIA SZMIT & HANNA DZIK	POL
2	NIA JERWOOD & LISA SMITH	AUS
3	MARIA CABA & CARLA DIAZ	ESP

Girl's Windsurfer - RS:X

1	STEFANIYA ELFUTINA	RUS
2	EMMA WILSON	GBR
3	XIAN TING HUANG	CHN

Boys Skiff - 29er

1	PETER LIN JANEZIC & ANZE PODLOGAR	SLO
2	JACKSON KEON & NICK EGNOT JOHNSON	NZL
3	TOMAS MATHISEN& MADS MATHISEN	NOR

Girls Skiff - 29er

1	SIRRE KRONLOF& VEERA HOKKA	FIN
2	LAERKE GRAVERSEN& IBEN NIELSBY CHRISTENSEN	DEN
3	GRETA STEWART& KATE STEWART	NZL

Open Mulithull - SL16

1	LOUIS FLAMENT & CHARLES DORANGE	FRA
2	SHAUN CONNOR & SOPHIE RENOUF	AUS
3	TAMRYN LINDSAY & WILLIAM MCKENZIE	NZL

Appendix B

Performance of ENP Participants at the Youth Sailing World Championships 2015

Name	Nat	Class	Pos
BLANCA VELASQUEZ	BIZ	Laser Radial Girls	43rd
FLORENCE ALLAN	CAY	Laser Radial Girls	26th
DANIELA RODRIGUEZ ORDONEZ	ECU	Laser Radial Girls	30th
PAIGE CLARKE	ISV	Laser Radial Girls	41st
KAITLYN DANIELLA DOUGLAS	TCA	Laser Radial Girls	45th
MEILING CHAN CHOW	TTO	Laser Radial Girls	48th
DOMINGAS HUAMBO	ANG	Laser Radial Girls	50th
NOUHA AKIL	ALG	Laser Radial Girls	38th
RWAN HASSAN	EGY	Laser Radial Girls	51st
ALISON HOAPEAU	SEY	Laser Radial Girls	53rd
CHUEH- YU CHOU	TPE	Laser Radial Girls	47th
ROSE-LEE NUMA	PNG	Laser Radial Girls	36th
ESTERE KUMPINA	LAT	Laser Radial Girls	39th
MARIA ERDI	HUN	Laser Radial Girls	1st
ROSE-LEE NUMA	PNG	Laser Radial Girls	36th
BIANCA LEILUA	SAM	Laser Radial Girls	37th
SYDNEY PETTITT	VAN	Laser Radial Girls	52nd
JULES MITCHELL	ANT	Laser Radial Boys	37th
SCOTT GITTENS	BAR	Laser Radial Boys	52nd
ANTONIO RICARDEZ	BIZ	Laser Radial Boys	58th
DANIEL PETROVIC	IVB	Laser Radial Boys	35th
MATIAS DYCK	ECU	Laser Radial Boys	11th
NOAH FURLONGE-WALKER	TTO	Laser Radial Boys	56th
FILIPE ANDRE	ANG	Laser Radial Boys	40th
SEDOUD SALIM	ALG	Laser Radial Boys	55th
ALI MOUTAZ ELDEMERDASH	EGY	Laser Radial Boys	61st
MARTIN SERVINA	SEY	Laser Radial Boys	64th
IMAMU SAID IMAMAU	TAN	Laser Radial Boys	63rd
SAIFEDINE DHOUADI	TUN	Laser Radial Boys	34th
CHI-CHIAN WU	TPE	Laser Radial Boys	48th
JAKUB HALOUZKA	CZE	Laser Radial Boys	20th
PATRIK MELIS	SVK	Laser Radial Boys	51st
JOSHUA LOANE	COK	Laser Radial Boys	53rd
TEARIKI NUMA	PNG	Laser Radial Boys	59th
MANU "BENNY" LORE	VAN	Laser Radial Boys	62nd
KHAIRUN HANNA MOHD AFENDY and SITI NUR FATIHAH NORULKHAIRI	MAS	420 Girls	16th
HARIS PAPAZOGLOU and RAFAEL THEOCHAROUS	CYP	420 Boys	25th
CHI-CHIAN WU and CHIH-YUAN CHU	TPE	420 Boys	30th
SIMON MARECEK and JAN SVOBODA	CZE	29er Boys	24th
ROBERTS JANIS VANCOVICS and EMILS UKASS	LAT	29er Boys	26th
MUHAMAD DHIAUDDIN ROZAINI and AHMAD LATIF MANSOR	MAS	29er Boys	31st
TOMAS BARRETO and JOAO PRIETO	POR	29er Boys	23rd

Christophe Launay

207

YOUTH WORLDS FACT SHEET

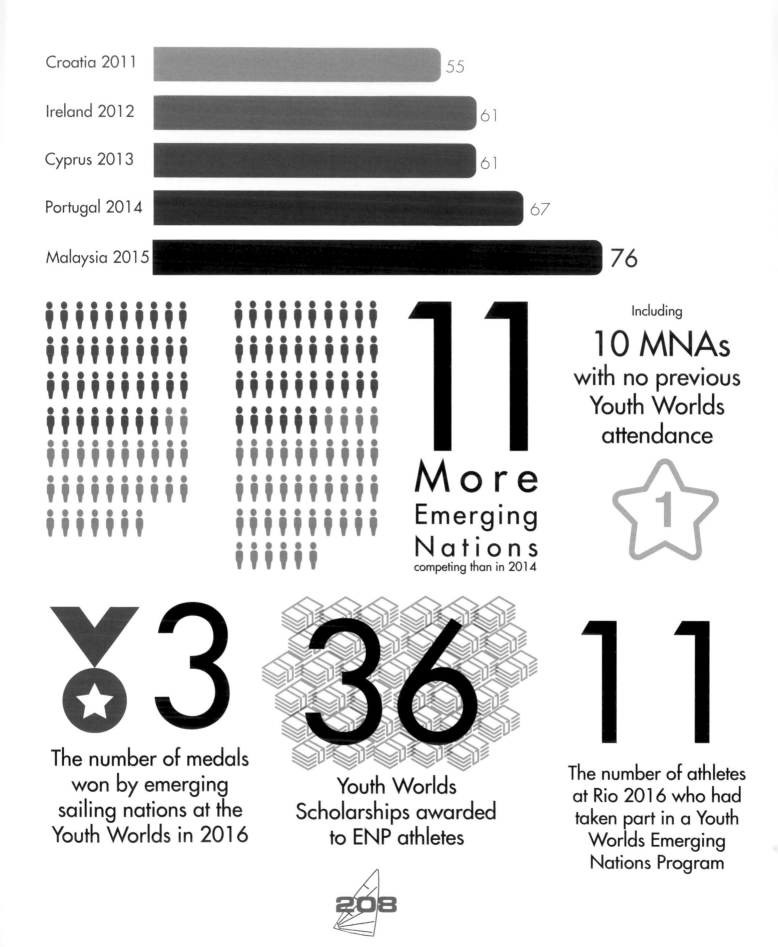

Croatia 2011 — 55
Ireland 2012 — 61
Cyprus 2013 — 61
Portugal 2014 — 67
Malaysia 2015 — 76

11
More Emerging Nations
competing than in 2014

Including
10 MNAs
with no previous Youth Worlds attendance
1

3
The number of medals won by emerging sailing nations at the Youth Worlds in 2016

36
Youth Worlds Scholarships awarded to ENP athletes

11
The number of athletes at Rio 2016 who had taken part in a Youth Worlds Emerging Nations Program

208

Christophe Launay

List of Emerging Nations 2015[*]

Asia			
Malaysia (MAS)	Sri Lanka (SRI)	Madagascar (MAD)	Guatemala (GUA)
Chinese Taipei (TPE)	**Thailand (THA)**	Malta (MLT)	Cayman Islands (CAY)
Pakistan (PAK)	United Arab Emirates (UAE)	Mauritius (MRI)	Trinidad and Tobago (TTO)
Kuwait (KUW)		Morocco (MAR)	Belize (BIZ)
Sri Lanka (SRI)	Africa	Nigeria (NGR)	Uruguay (URU)
Vietnam (VIE)	**Mozambique (MOZ)**	Senegal (SEN)	US Virgin Islands (ISV)
Bahrain (BRN)	Tanzania (TAN)	**South Africa (RSA)**	Ecuador (ECU)
Oman (OMA)	Angola (ANG)	Tanzania (TAN)	Bahamas (BAH)
I.R. Iran (IRI)	Seychelles (SEY)	Tunisia (TUN)	Bermuda (BER)
India (IND)	Algeria (ALG)	Uganda (UGA)	Grenada (GRN)
Indonesia (INA)	**Tunisia (TUN)**	Namibia (NAM)	Jamaica (JAM)
Iraq (IRK)	Sudan (SUD)		Netherlands Antillies (AHO)
Kyrgystan (KGZ)	Egypt (EGY)	Americas	Panama (PAN)
Myanmar (MYA)	Zimbabwe(ZIM)	Antigua (ANT)	Iceland (ISL)
Philippines (PHI)	Kenya (KEN)	Aruba (ARU)	**Mexico (MEX)**
Qatar (QAT)	Botswana (BOT)	British Virgin Islands (IVB)	Dominican Republic (DOM)
Saudia Arabia (KSA)	Djibouti (DJI)	Turks and Caicos (TKS)	Venezuela (VEN)
	Libya (LBA)	Barbados (BAR)	Nicaragua (NCA)

Daniel Forster

Paraguay (PAR)	Czech Republic (CZE)	Georgia (GEO)	Fiji (FIJ)
Columbia (COL)	Latvia (LAT)	Khazakstan (KAZ)	Guam (GUM)
Peru (PER)	Slovakia (SLO)	Kosovo(KOS)	Chinese Taipei (TPE)
El Salvador (ESA)	Bulgaria (BUL)	Lebanon (LIB)	Iran (IRI)
Puerto Rico (PUR)	**Cyprus (CYP)**	San Marino (SMR)	Myanmar (MYA)
St Kitts (skn)	Romania (ROM)	Serbia (SRB)	Vietnam (VIE)
St Vincent	**Portugal (POR)**	Slovak Republic (SLO)	American Samoa (ASA)
Columbia	**Israel (ISR)**	Belarus (BLR)	
St Lucia (LCA)	**Sweden (SWE)**	Estonia (EST)	
Tahiti (TAH)	**Lithuania (LTU)**	Slovenia (SLO)	
Chile (CHI)	Luxembourg (LUX)	Montenegro (MNT)	
Montenegro	Liechtenstein (LIE)	Palestine (PLE)	
Cuba (CUB)	Moldova (MDA)		
Uruguay (URU)	Iceland (ISL)	Oceana	Green - totally emerging programs.
	Macedonia (MKD)	Samoa (SAM)	Orange - countries whose
Europe	Andorra (AND)	Cook Islands (COK)	sailors occasionally made it to international events.
Hungary (HUN)	Armenia (ARM)	Vanuatu (VAN)	Red - Nations with an
Ukraine (UKR)	Azerbaijan (AZE)	Papua New Guinea (PNG)	established sailing program

* Classification circa Jan 2015

Appendix E

Athletes, Coaches, National Representitives & Media
Emerging Nations Program 2015

FIJI

Neville Koop (FIJ)	Sydney Pettitt (VAN)
Peter Thaleard (FIJ)	Manu "Benny" Lore (VAN)
Amanu Simpson (FIJ)	Graham Numa (PNG)
Gaby Stevens (FIJ)	Raymond Numa (PNG)
Naomi Waqalevu (FIJ)	Rose-Lee Numa (PNG)
Viliame Ratulu (FIJ)	Teariki Numa (PNG)
Derek Rawlinson (FIJ)	Sariva Keiloi (PNG)
Anne Tierney (COK)	Nynette Sass (SAM)
Titiroa "Ted" Tavai (COK)	Michael Rose (SAM)
Joshua Ioane (COK)	Bianca Leilua (SAM)
Helene Johnson (COK)	Diane Sharlene Gay (SAM)
Vanic Teina (COK)	Maria Anette Gay (SAM)
Paul Pettitt (VAN)	Victor Torres (GUM)
Benny Kaltonga (VAN)	Corey Santos (GUM)

ANTIGUA & BARBUDA

Geoffrey Pidduck (ANT)	Joselyn Echeverría Montesde Oca(GUA)
Shawn Ambrose (ANT)	Raphael Harvey (CAY)
Kelvin Brown (ANT)	Florence Allan (CAY)Pablo
Jalese Gordon (ANT)	Bertran (CAY)
Vincent Anfi (ANT)	James Arrindell (TTO)Christian
Jules Mitchell (ANT)	A. Chan Chow (TTO)
Rhone Kirby (ANT)	Noah Furlonge-Walker (TTO)
Julie Deakin (IVB)	Meiling Chan Chow (TTO)
Katelyn Woodman (IVB)	Andrew Milner (BIZ)
Jason Putley (IVB)	Trenton Miller (BIZ)
Daniel Petrovic (IVB)	Blanca Velasquez (BIZ)
David Douglas (TCA)	Antonio Ricardez (BIZ)
Daniella Kaitlyn Douglas(IVB)	Juan Luis Marabotto(URU)
Renata Goodridge (BAR)	Santiago Diz Becerra(URU)
Kwame Hinds (BAR)	Lyn Reid (ISV)
Scott Gittens (BAR)	Ian Liberty (ISV)
Alec Drayton (BAR)	Paige Clarke (ISV)
Monica Cofino (GUA)	Orlando Rodriguez (ECU)
Betina Litmanovich (GUA)	Jose Maria Sanchez Pagano(ECU)
Diego Silvestre Pérez (GUA)	Matias Dyck (ECU)

Photographer Chris Cameron
Videographer Yves Simard

Photographer Daniel Forster
Videographer Mike Audick

HUNGARY

András Holczhauser(HUN)
József Csomai (HUN)
Attila Regős (HUN)
Zsombor Majthényi (HUN)
Lili Kendeh (HUN)
Luca Kalmár
Liza Formanek (HUN)
Kristóf Ziegler (HUN)
Marcell Futó (HUN)
Lilla Takácsy (HUN)
Zsófia Varga (HUN)
Szebasztián Kálóczy (HUN)
Marai Erdi (HUN)
Attila Jámbor (HUN)
Ádám Csányi (HUN)
Mate Scharf (HUN)
Sergey Cherny (UKR)
Sergii Scherbakov (UKR)
Kateryna Gumenko (UKR)
Igor Lvov (UKR)
Illia Malovychko (UKR)
Dana Dvorakova (CZE)
David Krizek (CZE)
Simon Marecek (CZE)

Jan Svoboda (CZE)
Ingrida Krigere (LAT)
Zaklina Litauniece (LAT)
Roberts Janis Vancovis (LAT)
Emils Ukass (LAT)
Estere Kumpina (LAT)
Giedrius Alksnevicius (SVK)
Patrik Melis (SVK)
Lyubena Nacheva-Grigorova(BUL)
Stamo Tenev (BUL)
Plamen Yanakiev (BUL)
Marina Dimitrova (BUL)
Elena Papazoglou (CYP)
Nikolas Lofitis (CYP)
Haris Papazoglou (CYP)
Rafael Theocharous (CYP)
Radu Zitti (ROU)
Doara Liviu (ROU)
Zitti Andrei (ROU)
Pedro Rodrigues (POR)
Pedro Augusto Bolina (POR)
João Prieto (POR)
Tomás Barreto (POR)

Photographer Carlo Borlenghi
Videographer George Johns

MOZAMBIQUE

Helio Alberto Da Rosa (MOZ)
Adelino Reginaldo Maela (MOZ)
AndreAlexandreSilvaSanches(MOZ)
CesarAlexandreMorgadoSanches(MOZ)
Estaline Duarte (MOZ)
Antonio Freitas (MOZ)
AmadeAmadeAbdulAzizo Amade(MOZ)
Igor Perreira Inroga (MOZ)
Adriano Candido (MOZ)
Albamo Cardosa Magaia(MOZ)
Eurencio DinisNhanwave(MOZ)
Marcelino Jose Antonio(MOZ)
Edmilson Mandlate (MOZ)
Maria Mabjaia (MOZ)
Velick Manhica (MOZ)
Deurry Mavimbe (MOZ)
Miltom Magaia (MOZ)
Adolfo Novela (MOZ)
Armando Hochaha (MOZ)
Nelly Coelho(TAN)
Philemon Nassari (TAN)
Imamusaid Imamu (TAN)
Nganzi Mustafa (TAN)
Nuno Gomes (ANG)
Manuel Lelo (ANG)

Filipe André (ANG)
Domingas Huambo (ANG)
Alain Alcindor (SEY)
Allan Julie (SEY)
Alison Hoareau (SEY)
Martin Servina (SEY)
Joshua Confait (SEY)
Mourad Ouksoum (ALG)
Baraka Khereddine (ALG)
Boussouar Abdelkhalek (ALG)
Sedoud Salim (ALG)
Akil Nouha (ALG)
Karim Achour (TUN)
Hatem Rebaya (TUN)
Dhaouadi Saifeddine(TUN)
Houssem Bouafif (TUN)
M.hadi Karim (SUD)
Azzam Gaffhr Elhssan (SUD)
Eithar Azzan Gaffhr (SUD)
Mazen Mansour (SUD)
MahmoudAbu Elsaoud (EGY)
Mohamed GamalAbdelHalim(EGY)
Ali Moataz El-Demerdash (EGY)
Rawan Hossam Salama (EGY)
Mohannad Ayman Mohamed Abdelsalam (EGY)

Photographer Trevor Wilkins
Videographer Dan Haggett

YOUTH SAILING WORLD
CHAMPIONSHIP
-15

PNG

Christophe Launay

MALAYSIA

Abdullah MohdAfendy (MAS)
Norhisham Mat Nor (MAS)
Hamizatul Amirah Binti Hamdan(MAS)
Ahmad Khairulhafiz Bin Ahmad Khmbali (MAS)
Khairun Hanna Mohd Afendy (MAS)
Muhammad Danial Bin Shahidan (MAS)
Hsing-Ti Wu (TPE)
Chi-Chian Wu (TPE)
Chih-Yuan Chu (TPE)
Chueh-Yu Chou (TPE)
Commander Muhammad Akram Tariq (PAK)
Muhammad Azeem (PAK)

Muhammad Uzair (PAK)
Valentin Ivanov (KUW)
Ameena Shah (KUW)
Sarath Kuragama (SRI)
Welandagoda Pathiranage Krishan Janaka (SRI)
Anish Jayawardena (SRI)
Dinouk Goonewardana (SRI)
Nguyen Hai Duong (VIE)
Dung Tong Huu (VIE)
Nhi Pham Thi (VIE)
Trong Ta Ba (VIE)
Quynh Nguyen Van (VIE)

Photographer Christophe Launay
Videographer Stef Otto- Producer -Marcus Bailey

WORLD SAILING NOMINATED EXPERTS

Tim Cross (GBR)
Eduardo Sylvestre (BRA)
Pedro Rodrigues (POR)
Andrew Clouston (NZL)
Rob Holden(RSA)

420 Class Coach
Fernanda Sesto (ITA)

ADDITIONAL PHOTOGRAPHERS

Ashleigh de Villiers (RSA) - *Assistant to Trevor Wilkins*
Marcos Mendez(URU) - *Contents*
Ben Lovas (HUN) - *82/83*
Martin Allen (GBR) *202/203*
David Brannigan (IRL) - *216/217*
Daniel Smith (GBR) - *217*

Trevor Wilkins

Appendix F

The World Sailing Council 2012-2016

Front Row: Quanhai Li (CHN) - Vice-President, Chris Atkins (GBR) - Vice-President, Gary Jobson (USA) - Vice-President, Carlo Croce (ITA) - President, His Majesty King Constantine - President of Honour, Nazli Imre (TUR) - Vice-President, George Andreadis (GRE) - Vice-President, Adrienne Greenwood (NZL) - Vice-President, W. Scott Perrty (URU) - Vice-President

Row 2: L to R -Ross Robson (RSA), John Crebbin (IRL), Cory Sertl (USA), Kamen Fillyov (BUL), Peter Hall (CAN), Dick Batt (GBR), Dorith Stierler (ISR), David Tillett (AUS), Marijan Hanzekovič (CRO), Hector Duval (DOM) *seated*, Cary Lee Byerley (ANT), Tomasz Chamera (POL) *seated*, Ben Barger (USA), Abe Rosemberg (BRA) *no longer a Council member*, Khalifa M Al-Sewaidi (QAT).

Row 3: L to R - Totos Theodossiou (CYP), Jean-Pierre Champion, Rob Franken (NED), Loh Kok Hua (SIN), Karl C Kwok (HKG), Oleg Ilyan (RUS), Jeff Martin (GBR) - *Classes representative*, Pablo Masseroni (ARG).

Row 4: L to R - Rolf Bähr (GER) Kurt Lönnqvist (FIN) Gary Bodie (USA) Takao Otani (JPN) Rafael Gonzalez (ESP)

Not pictured: His Majesty King Harald V of Norway - President of Honour, Stig Hvide Smith (NOR), Georgy Shayduko (RUS), KokHua Loh (SIN), Jan Dawson (NZL), Hector Duval (DOM), Peter Hall (CAN), Stan Honey (USA), Jacques Lehn (FRA) - *Offshore representative*, Adrienne Cahalan (AUS) -*Women's representative*, Betsy Alison (USA), Sarah Gosling (GBR) - *Athlete's representative*.

Nazli Imre

Carlo Croce

From left: Scott Perry, Phillip Tolhurst, Christine Fox Taylor (*Mrs. Scott Perry*), Jenny Tolhurst, Lijia Xu, Quanhai Li

World Sailing President of Honor, His Majesty King Constantine (above), with Andrienne Greenwood (right) and Jan Dawson. At left: Maria Erdi is interviewed by Gary Jobson.

Trevor Wilkins